Suicide
or survival?

The challenge of the year 2000

Amadou-Mahtar M'Bow

Léon Boissier-Palun
Trygve Bratteli
Schuyler Chapin
Luis Echeverría
André Fontaine
Buckminster Fuller
Paolo Grassi
Jerzy Grotowsky
Oswaldo Guayasamín
Tewfik Al-Hakim
Han Suyin
Paul-Marc Henry
Michiko Inukai
Michel Jobert
Alfred Kastler
Vladimir Kemenov
Prem Kirpal
Tchavdar Kuranov
Takeo Kuwabara
Sean MacBride
Mircea Malitza
M. L. Mehrotra
Hephzibah Menuhin-Hauser
Philip Noel-Baker
Jean d'Ormesson
Alicia Penalba
Nancy Reeves
Janez Stanovnik
Tran Van Khe
Peter Ustinov
Bernard Zehrfuss

unesco

The opinions expressed in this work
are those of each author and are not
necessarily those of Unesco.

Published in 1978 by the
United Nations Educational, Scientific
and Cultural Organization
7 Place de Fontenoy, 75700 Paris
Printed by Journal de Genève (Suisse)

ISBN 92-3-101534-6 ✓

Suicide ou survie? Les défis de l'an 2000: 92-3-201534-X
Del temor a la esperanza. Los desafíos del año 2000: 92-3-301534-3

Printed in Switzerland

Titles in this series:

Preface

This work, the first of a series which Unesco plans to bring out on the major problems of our time, stems from a Round Table on 'The Challenge of the Year 2000'.

The breadth of this theme for reflection inevitably gave rise to highly complex approaches, from a variety of standpoints—economic, social, political, cultural, ethical, etc.—since the problems dealt with proved to be closely interdependent, reflecting the actual pattern of the order—or disorder—which is a feature of our society in this last quarter of the twentieth century.

The very wealth of contributions from the various participants, scholars, artists, philosophers and politicians, all expressing themselves in accordance with one or other different schools of thought, made it necessary to classify them under a few major headings by way of a guide to the reader.

The work is therefore divided into four organic sections. 'Man—Puppet or Master of Own His Achievements', 'Man against the Powers that Be', 'A New Social Contract' and 'The Continuing Battle of Culture', within which each contribution relates to others, converging with, or diverging from them in the kind of polyphonic mode which invested the discussions with such originality and depth.

Notes in the margin have been added to explain certain allusions or provide a reference background.

Contents

The challenge of the year 2000

Amadou Mahtar M'Bow
Director-General of Unesco

A year ago, a number of outstanding personalities from all the main regions of the world and with every sort of cultural background attended a first Round Table meeting in this building on 'Cultural and Intellectual Co-operation and the New International Economic Order'.

I am glad to see several of last year's participants here again today, together with a number of eminent figures in science, education, culture and communication.

To all of you who have answered the appeal from Jean d'Ormesson, the Secretary-General of the International Council for Philosophy and Humanistic Studies, whom I should like to thank publicly on behalf of the Organization, I extend a most hearty welcome to Unesco. Please make yourselves at home in this building; and please, of course, carry on your discussions with complete and absolute freedom. I hardly need to emphasize the interest with which we shall follow this meeting, or the importance we attach to your deliberations: for the topic you have to consider is nothing less than the future of mankind over the next quarter of a century.

The subject of this year's Round Table is, as you know, 'The Challenge of the Year 2000'.

I would not, in any way, anticipate your deliberations. I imagine, however, that you will not confine yourselves merely to identifying the various aspects of the challenge—though even that would be an achievement. You will presumably also (without undue recourse to the crystal ball) be at pains to suggest, not of course magical panaceas, but at any rate possible methods of meeting the challenge as human beings. For the challenge is not to 'man' as an abstract entity, but to all men and women, rich or poor, in both the northern and southern hemispheres; and it is upon us here and now.

The fate of all the nations of the world is so closely linked (though each of them very properly expects to be treated as an individual entity) that 'here' in the previous sentence must be understood as encompassing the whole globe. 'Now', covering the space of the next twenty-five years, represents no more than a fleeting glimpse in relation to the cavalcade of human history; but the way this glimpse is focused and angled will determine the fate of our children and grandchildren, and perhaps even the general tenor of the twenty-first century. It is certainly true that peoples make their own history, and it would be presumptuous of the present generation to project its own history into the future and expect to influence the lives of generations yet to come. But the process of change which the world is undergoing is so rapid and so complex that decisions taken and choices made today can permanently affect the future. Moreover, if mankind is to live in peace and harmony, all the men and women who constitute it must realize what changes are needed both in the way they organize their own lives and the way they envisage their relations with others.

It is commonly said that we are entering on an era of interdependence between peoples, and that from now on no one nation will be able to live and prosper without taking account of the others. This *de facto* interdependence, which favours some at the expense of others, must now be transmuted into a genuine joint responsibility for a common destiny.

This, to my mind, is one of the great issues of our time: and I believe that, in the course of your deliberations, in addition to considering the world in which we each of us live our lives today, you might well extrapolate its future— always remembering our essential community of interests. Any approach confined to one aspect only of present-day development, without taking realistic and comprehensive account of the diversity of the human race and its aspirations, would be liable to give a wholly false picture of today's world, and of tomorrow's too.

May I tentatively suggest one or two other questions that might, if you think it appropriate, be worth considering during your discussion?

The first concerns the idea of development itself, and the divisions that unequal development produces between the so-called developed industrialized countries and the so-called developing ones: the latter being characterized by inadequate mastery of science and technology in industrial production and social organization. It has long been thought that the development model proposed by the most highly industrialized countries was the ideal, and that all societies were bound to follow the same course. Nowadays, much of the accepted wisdom on this subject is being questioned. It may be that we should investigate further the approach adopted by those other peoples who, while not achieving the level of material development of the industrialized world, have always believed the ultimate end of all production to be the promotion of the complete fulfilment of man in all his varied aspirations. I think that this might help to further the discussion as a whole. Another question arises directly from this 'methodological doubt' which I have allowed myself to express to you so freely—but here I am only setting the example for that free thinking which I am sure will be a feature of this meeting, as it was of last year's.

This second question concerns people's relationships with one another, and the individual's relationship with the group. This brings us to the idea of democracy itself, the denial of which (as the preamble to Unesco's Constitution emphasizes) made possible the Second World War.

If we want twenty-first-century men and women to enjoy a degree of happiness over and above the mere daily struggle against hunger—still all too onerous a task for the majority of the world's inhabitants—and to achieve their full potential, the time has perhaps come to concentrate all our efforts in the field of social organization on greater and more genuine participation by individuals in decision-making.

I am of course meticulously careful to abide by the principle that our Organization 'is prohibited from intervening in matters which are essentially within [the] domestic jurisdiction' of Member States—that is from paragraph 3 of Article I of our Constitution; but paragraph 1 of the same article states that the purpose of the Organization is 'to contribute to peace and security ... in order to further universal respect for justice, for the rule of law and for the human rights and fundamental freedoms which are affirmed for the peoples of the world...'.

This question of respect for human rights, which is very topical today, is not a new one in our Organization; but I am delighted to see that it is engaging the attention of an ever-growing number of people. We can never hope to carry out a wide-ranging campaign without the support of those most concerned.

No less important a concept is that of active participation by the peoples of the world, at all social levels, in the life of their own countries. Here I am thinking of the part to be played by international non-governmental organizations, in parallel with intergovernmental organizations like Unesco, and also, in each country, by private societies and voluntary bodies engaged in research on the environment, consumer affairs, social and economic justice, and the social responsibilities of business concerns. I accordingly ask you who are specialists, each in your own field, to devote some thought to a specific aspect of the challenge: namely how these pressing contemporary problems can cease to be the exclusive preserve of specialists. What I am really asking you to contemplate is a sort of 'realist Utopia': democracy in a society without cut-throat competition. At the ordinary everyday level, this might enable men and women at last to live really happily with others. At world level, it could only lead to the 'new international order' which Unesco is anxious to help introduce.

I realize that this presupposes peaceful coexistence as between different social and cultural systems, and the unreserved acceptance of these differences: i.e. respect for the other man's cultural identity. Above all it presupposes an international consensus on something that is not so much a life-style as a code for coexistence. By guaranteeing peace and the survival of generations yet unborn, by giving real meaning once again to the idea of solidarity in a world full of diverse but interdependent problems, this new order would surely reconcile humanity with itself.

I call upon you to help us carry forward our thinking in the light of the fact that the twenty-first century is already almost upon us.

Man—puppet
or master of his own
achievements

First, a revolution in thinking

Luis Echeverría

We live at a critical period and words must be filled with real meaning if they are to recover their creative power and their capacity to bring men together. I consider it essential, philosophically and politically speaking, that words and deeds should be matched and merged as fire combines with air in common action.

This necessity is not a literary creation; it is, on the contrary, by virtue of the immense seriousness of the problems which surround us, a question of an inexorable law for survival.

At the beginning of the century, which seemed to bring with it the panacea of irreversible progress, the population of the world did not exceed 1,620 million. Within the space of seventy-seven years, we have gone past 4,000 million and on the most optimistic hypothesis, we shall have reached about 7,000 million by the end of the twentieth century.

Latin America, which in 1824, at the end of her wars of independence had less than 30 million inhabitants, has already exceeded 320 million and will have more than 600 million when we come to the end of this century. A century which has seen, at the same time, the explosion of the atomic bomb and the unspeakable and intolerable poverty of hundreds of millions of human beings. That is our common historical ground. But it in no way rules out the possibility of a true and profound transformation of the world. This hope is based neither on mere words without practice, nor on pure, anarchic action which eliminates the revolutionary role of organized intelligence in the service of our peoples.

When I speak of hope, I am referring to the hope which is the fruit of historical action by men and women, to hope built upon a concrete, objective plan for changing—by means of a new world economic order—the present state of injustice and the tragic squandering of resources. We must remember that, at the beginning of this century, a large part of the political geography of the world was still colonial. If this century already occupies a decisive place in the history of humanity, it will be precisely for that reason, because in the reconquest of historical initiative and the recovery of freedom and sovereignty there can now be no turning back, no undoing of what has been done in historical and social terms. This process, which is irreversible, will continue until all men and all nations have achieved complete liberation.

But this great fact of decolonization has made clear to us what the ideology of imperial power caused us not to see in the previous period, the colonial phase—the extent of exploitation in the world, the extent of the gulf between poverty and affluence.

This dual phenomenon has continued, to become a material fact, indisputable, clear and explicit today. It takes the form of a new will to dominate by other means. It constitutes the most unequivocal proof of the fundamental irrationality of a development model whose extraordinary potential for expansion and the transformation of nature is based on increasing the distance and widening the gulf between those who have nothing and those who have everything.

The internal dynamics of that process of growth and poverty will be modified only by two means: by the historical action of nations and by the decision of intelligence organized as a critical weapon, as a social conscience, as an irresistible means of change. This enormous subject is of direct concern to Unesco, the world centre in which the nations are gathered together.

This is because intelligence, organized, structured and systematized in scientific knowledge, based on the standards of reason and of ethics, cannot, without courting self-destruction, be used for the purposes of an economic and scientific model based on irrationality and irresponsibility.

This historical contradiction has been brought about not only by the appropriation of the material resources of humanity by tiny minorities in the world, but also by the systematic appropriation of science and scientists for the profit and power of monopoly groups or superpowers.

The decolonization of the colonial world was an undertaking which dominated human imagination from the first appearance of oppression and domination throughout that human adventure which has been called the quest for liberty.

The decolonization of science and intelligence from an ethnocentric situation benefiting only the few, represents the most revolutionary, radical and imperative undertaking for the last quarter of this century.

Not only because the world is faced with the possibility of the exhaustion of the non-renewable natural resources which were the age-old heritage of humanity. Not only because of the terrible risks of the arms race. Not only for these reasons. I should say, in the face of so many documents and studies predicting the end of non-renewable natural resources, that such an interpretation, apparently scientific, is nothing less than an ideological interpretation. Still further, I should say that such an interpretation is, on whatever subject, a false ideology. A false ideology in the service of the very interests which, having founded their wealth on waste and the squandering of the earth's resources, seek now to establish a supra-scientific monopoly over the new sources of energy and the new alternatives which science will make feasible.

Human knowledge converted into the possibility of producing rational alternatives to problems, cannot be appropriated and reified for the service once more of a model of development which, in the technocratic phase of power, would increase the gulf between peoples and, consequently, make international relations more explosive.

I call therefore for the critical break made in full consciousness of its consequences, with models of knowledge which tend to reproduce irrationality when they could bring with them the revolution of intelligence. If the new forms of energy, if our new human resources, become once more the birthright of a minority of peoples and social classes, the twenty-first century will inevitably become a scene set for a possible atomic apocalypse: an assumption based on a rigorous analysis of contemporary society. To put it clearly and simply: if the economic and political objectives of the next decades were to be concentrated, once more, on military and scientific rivalry, instead of on peaceful co-operation and a pooling of knowledge, humanity would find itself in a nuclear deadlock. It is consequently essential to make a complete, historical break with our present way of thinking. We must integrate scientific knowledge, and the scientists, in a cultural revolution which seeks, by the application of criticism, to bring about change in the goals of development. A psychological and sociological transformation in their own situation as the representatives and exponents of a science which has been separated from the higher, universal aims of the world's peoples.

At this moment, the richer 19 per cent of the earth's population controls 64.5 per cent of the world's gross national product. On the other hand, 1,400 million of its inhabitants, representing seventy nations with 32.6 per cent of the population of the planet, control a mere 4.4 per cent of the total wealth.

Can such a situation continue and even worsen?

Setting aside any sort of ethical consideration and viewing the matter without any metaphysical pretension, it appears obvious not only that this situation is intolerable, but that it acts dynamically as a factor of conflict, as a gigantic social cancer destroying world balance, at one and the same time, for the most privileged and for the most deprived. No single problem can be detached, nowadays, from the overall picture of mankind as a whole.

Among the nations of the Third World, according to official sources, unemployment at present affects 300 million people. Peripheral development, associated with the aims of metropolitan development, is transforming this present-day problem into a gigantic problem for tomorrow. Especially since the demographic explosion is accompanied by, and superimposed on, the urban explosion. In 1950, only 39 per cent of the population of Latin America, for example, could be classified as urban; the figure will be 73 per cent by the year 2000, and 80 per cent for the world as a whole.

The problems of employment, housing, education, health and food will take on a radically explosive character which neither guns nor demagogues will be able to eliminate.

What we need to do is to give effect, on an enormous scale, to coherent, logical, interdependent answers.

The solution of the problem is not to be found in the verbal Utopia produced by a childish radicalism, of an equitable statistical redistribution of the world's wealth. The true answer lies in the rational use of material resources, human resources and scientific knowledge as qualitative, revolutionary instruments of change.

For this very reason, I call upon organized intelligence in universities, laboratories, institutes and centres of learning to effect the historic recovery of its own critical autonomy, that is, to achieve its own ethnocentric decolonization, in order to lay the foundations for a real and fruitful dialogue among civilizations, bypassing all monopolies.

Alienation and the sense of estrangement have become established in the field of science, converting it into an industry, and that industry of knowledge into a military, industrial and academic complex whose dynamic development is no longer controlled or governed by its own creators and inventors.

At this moment the world spends about $350,000 million on arms: a figure higher than the gross national product of Latin America, an amount twenty-six times greater than the government aid which the richest countries in the world granted the Third World in 1975.

The lack of proportion between means and ends, and the inequality in the goals set are so absolute as to make partial solutions, whether honest or dishonest, unviable. The material failure of the latest international conferences, including the Paris conference on co-operation, reveals not only that there is no desire to change, but what is worse, that the systems of organized intelligence are used as instruments in the service of a power economy still based, instinctively, on primary accumulation, the power of armed strength, and total lack of responsibility as regards the very consequences of scientific knowledge, which should always aim, inexorably, at the liberation of man. The Third World is neither a semantic invention nor an ideological invention of the laboratory. Underdevelopment has been built up, stone by stone, by the mechanisms of development. In short, it is not possible to separate out the world economic model or to isolate peripheral and central zones, as if we were dealing with spheres in a laboratory. Both form part of a single economic and social structure. The twenty-three remaining years of this century must be devoted to the establishment of a new world economic order. The population of the Third World represents, at present, three out of four human beings. By the year 2000, taking the hypothesis of a total population of 6,900 million, 5,400 million inhabitants will belong to the Third World. By the year 2018, when the world's population will have doubled, out of a possible total population of 9,710 million, 7,730 million inhabitants would belong to the Third World.

It is idle, in the face of this rising tide, to contemplate a desperate and useless attempt at mass sterilization. We must aim, in human, scientific and rational terms, at a qualitative transformation of life which will affect population growth at its very root: that is to say, underdevelopment.

We cannot talk of freedom and education in the setting of unequal development and irrationality in the goals of mankind. Freedom cannot be expressed as the privilege of a few, but as the creation of human community of free men. And no community of free men can be based, indefinitely, on the exploitation, poverty and ignorance of the majorities. History, our mother and teacher, has always brought this home to us with blood, pain and tears.

If we do not wish, by the year 2000, to make hunger and social poverty the common denominator of a failed civilization, we shall have to organize our human and scientific resources by reference to a new criterion. Transcending the usual exponential extrapolations from the economic crisis, I would here call for a mental revolution, that is, a scientific revolution which will bring together those who work on behalf of organized intelligence to serve our peoples, and not an irrational system, tragically erected in opposition to the very essence of scientific reason.

Humanity is, at this moment, in possession of the greatest store of knowledge ever witnessed in the course of history.

This gigantic accumulation of knowledge has the infrastructures and the equipment to change the world. To achieve and secure this change, we need not a mythical revolution, but an objective and profound revolution which will reconcile man's survival and truly human development with the conquest of liberty.

The wealth that makes men poor

Janez Stanovnik

The generation that separates us from the second millennium is a relatively short period in history. Nevertheless, I think that within that generation quite a lot will happen and, to illustrate the case, I would like to invite you on a very short trip into the past with me. I invite you back to the year 1950 to examine with me how 1975–77 looked from the perspective of 1950. The generation just emerging then was to see the world's population increase by more than 1,500 million people. Let me remind you that 1,500 million people was the total population of the globe at the beginning of this century. In the course of one generation, we were, as of 1950, to see the production of goods and services multiplied by three. May I remind you that humanity needed a few hundred thousand years to reach the level of the gross national product by 1950 which, in one generation only, was to be trebled. During this period of twenty-five years we used just about four times more unrenewable geochemically stored energy resources, that is, about three to four times more than we were using in 1950. And may I remind you that this figure, trebled over a twenty-five-year period, adds up to the total value and the total volume of energy consumed by humanity since its inception! May I further remind you that in 1950 we had only 50 million cars but that, before this generation has lived out its time, there will be 250 million cars on the roads. In the same period, the merchant marine will quadruple the number of ships and the amount of housing will also increase four times.

Everything was to grow fantastically and in fantastic proportions. There were to be other changes, remarkable

progress in science. The genetic code was to be broken and
man was to step upon the moon, defying the law of gravity.
He was to encircle the globe with satellites and the world was
suddenly to be able to hear and see everything instantly.
Last but not least, in one generation we were to witness the
end of colonial rule.   United Nations membership was to
increase from 50 to about 150, to mention just a few things
that were to occur during this twenty-five-year period.

Alas, not all was to be to the good because there were to
be very great problems along with these tremendous achievements of civilization.   Inequality among men was to be
greatly accentuated. We, here in the developed world, were
to increase our total production three to four times over.
And let me remind you that the increment of our production
was to be just about five times greater than the total production of the less-privileged part of the world. We were
to be using resources in undreamed-of amounts, so that
the balance between man and nature was dangerously threatened, bringing us into totally new kinds of conflict. And,
just as production and everything else was to increase, so did
the conflicts among men. There were to be wars, very nasty
wars, and there were some other paradoxical developments
with the armament race for instance, bringing détente in its
wake. We were also to have during this twenty-five-year
period a conference on security and co-operation in Europe.[1]

At present I must ask why things are as they are. Why
have they happened this way? When we started our trip in
1950, world relations were such that the social and political
power of the working class (everybody understands, of
course, that I am a Marxist) was considerable and the power
of the primary producers was very weak.

The result of this was that the developed world was to
make ample use of cheap primary products, particularly
energy and very sparing use of manpower because it was
expensive and was to get more and more expensive. Wages
were to increase and with wages inflation was to increase as
well. In the developed part of the world a kind of technological civilization was accordingly to be achieved by 1975
which was extremely high in productivity but which would
shape society in such wise that the proportion of the population servicing the manufacturing industries would remain
almost stable. About one-quarter of the labour force was to
be employed in manufacturing, with little change in that
figure over the years.

One the one hand, there was to be an increase in services
and most particularly a booming expansion of bureaucracy
and administration. This constituted the sociological picture   *1* Helsinki, August 1975.

2 Growth is a recent world phenomenon affecting the whole of mankind. It is expressed in terms of two factors: population and gross national product. There are two driving forces behind growth. The first is population increase, which provides both producers and consumers, and the second is the sum of scientific advances and technological innovations leading to industrialization and the consumer society.

Growth policies are initially determined by factors of scarcity and urgency, as in the case of eighteenth-century Europe and the developing countries today. Since 1945, and in different circumstances, the same has applied to Western Europe, the socialist countries, China and Japan.

Growth is a major objective for the Third World. The purposes of growth, however, are ill-determined and its limits hazy. In addition to which, accumulated leeway and ever-increasing inequalities compromise growth. The 'for or against growth' issue involves three attitudes towards the development of industrial society:

Continue at all costs and
    even accelerate growth.
    Science will find solutions,
    fresh resources, etc.

Slow down growth and
    strike a balance between
    consumption and invest-
    ment, duration of work
    and technical progress,
    the international environ-
    ment and economic
    behaviour patterns.

Put an immediate stop to
    growth. This is the
    position of the advocates
    of zero economic growth.
    As they see it, growth
    merely results in a point-
    less accumulation of
    material goods and leads
    the world to disaster.

3 *The Future of the World Economy*, a United Nations study by Wassily Leontief *et al.*, Oxford University Press, 1977. Prepared by a

of developed societies by 1975. On the other hand, the developing countries which were to forge ahead during this quarter-century were to follow very much the pattern of so-called transfer of technology, hence also transfer of the developmental model. Therefore, some developing countries were also to experience growth. Statistics recorded this growth, a growth largely of products manufactured by companies transferred from the developed part of the world. Accordingly, this increase in production was recorded geographically as well. But how is it that the poor in these countries were to become poorer and the rich richer, not only in the world at large, but in the developing countries? The reason for this is that this growth pattern does not affect societies, it remains isolated in watertight compartments; there is growth, but not change. It is not development, it is just growth. [2] Therefore, we have a statistical geographic increase of products and services but no social transformation. Now, with this statement, let us look into the future. It would be very pretentious for me to try to do this alone. People far more learned than I have done it. Leontief, a Nobel Prize winner, recently wrote for the United Nations his study on the future of world economy. [3] I may have quarrels with some of his points but what I do not take issue with is the most professional way in which he assembled incontestable statistical figures. Now, the conclusion he reaches is that, whatever assumptions you make, even if you assume that the developed world will grow from now on much more slowly than it did in the past, not by 5 but by 3 per cent, the general and per capita income of the developed world will still be trebled taking account of its reduced population growth. While in the developing world, in absolute terms, the growth of income will be much faster than in the developed world there will be a considerable lag as a result of the population growth which cannot be much less than 2 to 2.5 per cent. The developing countries, particularly the poorest among them, may add some $50–$70 to the per capita income during this twenty-five-year period while the developed countries, on the average, may add between $2,000 and $3,000 per capita. The inequalities will accordingly grow considerably. Even though Leontief postulates statistically an overall reduction of existing inequalities from 1 to 12 to 1 to 7, this aim could only be achieved if those among the developing countries which are more richly endowed with natural resources grow much faster than those who so badly need them and those who cannot obtain them. Therefore, though this projection postulates greater equality, when more deeply analysed, it reveals new kinds of inequalities hidden beneath these laudable attempts to reduce the original ones. I am constrained then to ask the following question: what about resources? Now here Leontief's input–output projection shows that, if we continue as we did in the past, I mean all of humankind, developed and less developed, we will quadruple the consumption of geochemical energy from just about the equivalent of 6,000 million tons of coal to something very close to 30,000 million tons. Leontief adds that, in this way, we will use up three to four times as much ore and energy as humanity has used throughout its entire history! [4] Is this conceivable? Is this moral? Can we, one generation out of thousands of generations, take the liberty of using up what nature has been storing not only for us but for those who will come after us? Can we really behave in such a completely irresponsible way? But I will go a step further because this projection shows that we, in the developed world, will not be satisfied with only one car per two people as in the United States of America but will tend to quadruple our quota of cars. Why? Why would I need three cars? We cannot go on for another generation in the same way as we did for the last one. We cannot for two reasons: because, in the developed world it is impossible and because others in the developing world do not wish to do it. We must consider other models, other choices open to all of us. I view the developments from now to the end of this century under one simple slogan of equality. There must be greater equality between nations and peoples. How is this to be achieved? I think that in the developed world people will behave, as they say, rationally (not because people are moral; I do not believe in morality, I take people as they are; I do not try to paint them better than they are). To behave rationally is to serve their own self-interest. People in the developed world in the name of self-interest will be compelled to change their style of life because over-consumption is nauseating. People will gradually realize that material goods are not everything. Gradually humanity will realize that frantic consumption in one generation will leave nothing for posterity. I am, therefore, optimistic. I believe that the structure of employment will move toward more than just bureaucratic services and that man, who does not live by bread alone, will devote more resources to science, education and culture in general. I believe that the style of live in the developed world will become less materialistic than it is today, and that greater weight will be given to cultural creation and therefore to the structure of employment. Statisticians will show us that the rate of growth has dropped abruptly because they measure growth only in material

team of eminent economists under the direction of Wassily Leontief, Nobel Prize winner in economics (1973), this work describes the economic and political measures needed to establish the new international economic order, which has been a major United Nations objective since 1974.

The major problems of the next twenty-five years concern: the feeding of a more and more rapidly growing world population; the energy resources required for accelerated development; the serious effects of pollution on economic growth and development. On their solution depends a more even distribution of the world's wealth. What is needed is to reduce the tremendous gap between rich and poor regions in the world.

This highly scientific study, the most painstaking and thorough so far carried out, by means of an innovative econometric technique (input-output) which we owe to Leontief, draws optimistic conclusions. The limits to growth are dependent on political and social factors and on economic situations the modification of which will alone make it possible to end underdevelopment.

4   According to Leontief (*The Future of the World Economy*), the world increase in consumption of mineral resources will be enormous: 4.8 times for copper, 4.2 times for bauxite and zinc, 4.3 times for nickel, 5.3 times for lead and iron ore, 4.7 times for petroleum, 5.2 times for natural gas, 4.5 times for coal, etc. Despite new, more rational and more economical methods of using mineral resources, it is to be expected that, over, the next thirty years, the world will consume between three and four times the volume of minerals it has used up since the dawn of civilization.

products. There will be fewer material products, but there will be more of other valuable things which cannot be statistically measured. How can you measure the value of beautiful pictures? How can you measure the most beautiful music? They do not fit into the gross national product. There will be more of these statistically imponderable elements in the production of the more developed world. I think that the new international economic order is not just a slogan. We mean it. We mean it as much as President Roosevelt meant the New Deal[5] when his country was in the depths of the worst depression it had known. And what the developing countries are asking for with the new international economic order is nothing else but a New Deal for the world. Now what was the secret of the New Deal? The secret was that there were unemployed people, there were unemployed machines, and unused natural resources. All this had to be put into operation again, so production started with people earning salaries again, living once more, experiencing well-being. What we have today is world-wide unemployment, with natural resources lying fallow. There must, therefore, be world-wide action for putting to productive use all the resources which are currently idle. And this, I believe, has to be done and will be done, not because people are good but because they are egotists. The people in the developed world who are caught today between unemployment and inflation, have learned during the last two years that there is no solution within the economies of the developed world that does not also include a solution for international world economy. The way out of the present stagnation is a large-scale world-wide programme, a new deal for the world. Is all this realistic? Because you see it was quite easy for Marx in the middle of the last century to predict a socialistic society in the world, because he ascribed to the social and political force which was the working class a historical mission—that of transforming society into a socialist society in its own self-interest. This was his prediction 150 years ago.

Now, today, I would be more careful in putting such exclusive trust into any one identifiable social group. I would put greater trust in something I will term the counter-vailing power which is as universally true in human society as it is in nature, namely the fact that things cannot go beyond certain limits. There must accordingly be a major change, because I think that in many areas we have gone beyond the limit and I, like every economist, every sociologist and other specialist, have a theory as to why things are not better than they theoretically should be. There must be a basic change because in so many sectors we have come to

5 The New Deal was the policy of social and economic reforms advocated by Roosevelt when he became President of the United States in 1932 to deal with a disastrous situation which had been steadily worsening since the major crisis of 1929. There were then over 15 million unemployed in the United States. Agricultural prices had slumped and there was much the same picture of poverty in both town and country. The New Deal comprised a whole series of measures to increase purchasing power (higher wages and salaries, higher payments to farmers, cheaper manufactured goods, unemployment benefits, etc.) and to set on foot major State-sponsored construction schemes. The interventionism of the New Deal was condemned in 1935–36 by the Supreme Court, which declared various very important laws unconstitutional. It nevertheless modified the structures of American society, developed federal administration and aided the establishment of trade unions.

the end of the line. I do very firmly believe that this basic
change must be on a global scale, that will be gradual, with
an accompanying de-emphasis of material goods, in the
coming twenty-five years. It is becoming apparent already.
I believe that the growth pattern or transfer of growth from
the developed world into the developing one will cease and
true development will come from growth *with* change.
Intrinsically, societies will not only produce more but they
will also undergo social change and this is what makes me
optimistic in the long run.

π or the triumph of intelligence

Buckminster Fuller

My experience has been such that I now know that humanity has some extremely important options: including the option to really make it on this planet, which can be done within critical time-limits. I do not know that humanity is going to do it at all, whether humanity is going to exercise those options. I think it is so touch-and-go every minute that I feel very deeply responsible in being allowed to express an opinion about those options.

I know that we have the options. I am saying this as an engineer, speaking entirely from experience and I am not using opinion at all. But to know that we have options is anything but being an optimist. I think we must make this distinction. Because I have been able to make clear to really quite large numbers of human beings that we do have options, those people who did not know that we had options before tend to feel better and then they say that my optimism has rubbed off on them so that I find that I do get confused with being an optimist: I am anything but. I would like to list these options which we have. Fifty years ago this year, at the age of 32, I decided to make an experiment—turn my life into an experiment: to see what a little individual, without money, without credit, might be able to do on behalf of all humanity which great power structures, such as great corporations and great political States, might not be able to do, in fact, could not do. It was perfectly clear to me at the outset that, as three-quarters of the earth was covered with water, the amount of land that the great political world States really commanded was relatively limited. They might have allies but still they would be very limited, and all of the great corporations were limited too; they too must spread themselves and think, otherwise they would go broke; and all the great heads of corporations had to make a profit within a very few years or they would lose their jobs.

The heads of political States had to be able to maintain their positions, so they were always being inherently short-sighted. They were forced to be short-sighted. And there was nothing to stop the little individual thinking about our planet as a space-ship and thinking about it in the terms of the total knowledge that is acquired by humans; thinking about the total resources; trying to think about, as I tried to do, why humans were born on this planet, why are we present here in the universe, and trying to understand what we might do with those resources and knowledge to make humans a success on this planet as it seems we must have been designed to be. I began then thinking in very long terms and I undertook a fifty-year prognostication in 1927. I am quite confident that most of what I was able to foresee in 1927 has come into clear view today as possibly extremely relevant. How did I carry it out having no money? Obviously, with the billions of human beings on board our planet and my life expectancy at that time only another ten years (life expectancy when I was born was 42 and I was 32), I realized I was not going to get anywhere trying to persuade people about anything. I could see, however, that nature is always in transformation, always in evolution. I tried to understand the evolutionary significance of our being here and then tried to understand the total purport of life on our planet where you and I, requiring a great deal of energy, cannot take it through our own skins. It all comes from the sun. We cannot take it directly through our skins, so all the vegetation, all the algae in the sea and all vegetation on dry land were designed to impound that sun radiation by photosynthesis, convert it into useful hydrocarbons to be consumed by other creatures. I saw then that the vegetation, being exposed to all that radiation, had to have roots so that it could not be knocked over when the winds were blowing and had to have water out of the ground to give it its actual structural strength; and had to also have a water system that valved the water so that you could get it back in the sky, rain it back on the vegetation to keep the vegetation growing.

Because all the vegetation was rooted, it could not reach other vegetation to procreate. What nature had done was to invent all kinds of little mobile creatures, flying creatures, crawling creatures and so forth, and to design them to traffic back and forth between the vegetation to inadvertently cross-pollinate them, so that the vegetation would keep on growing.

In order to be able to get those little creatures to do what they did, nature had given them chromosomic programming, so that, say, the honey-bee would go after its honey—flower after flower—inadvertently knocking off pollen at ninety-degree angles.

I saw that humanity was thinking in small stages. Having been born naked, helpless and ignorant, and in due course having discovered some principles and learned to domesticate some animals, it had come to the point where one man could successfully herd milk-cows into full growth and another man had learned how to make shoes. Now the man with the cow wanting a pair of shoes, they talked with one another and realized there was more time involved in raising the cow than there was in the making of the shoes, and that you could not cut up cows to get shoes; so men invented money as a way of equating these odd inputs of time and competence on the part of the grower, or the producer. We then had money and I see human beings today as honey-money-bees going after their money, doing all the right things for the wrong reasons with this as part of the game-rules of how to carry on. Ecology was the main show and these little drives were all the side-effects required to make the total system coherent.

I decided then I must think if I were to commit myself to developing artefacts concerned with life-support and employing the highest knowledge that human beings have as well as the highest production capabilities—all of which is now being assigned the highest priority in national defence. Our great nations operate on the basis of the working assumption of a fundamental inadequacy of life-support on our planet: you may not like our system but we have the fairest, most logical, most ingenious way of coping. But, because there are those who disagree completely with our method of coping, it can only be resolved by trial of arms. Which is the fittest system to survive?

And we have then all these great national defence commitments, fundamental mandates of heads of States, to use the most vital resources exclusively for preparing defence or saying that a good offence is a better defence, but continually monopolizing resources, whether it be helium or one of the chemical elements that may be combined to high advantage in making alloys. They are relatively scarce. Who has access to them? The military, of course. And then, as the military always has the highest priority, you have to have anti-priorities, so the anti-priorities have always been the home front. The working substances are nowhere near adequate for all humanity anyway. We men are going to have to die anyway. So let the home front make do with low-performance materials or no performance at all. Our whole world of architecture, etc., is related then to the non-high performance, with the exception of the fortress idea of sheer bulk, deepness and heaviness that convinced man that he was safe until the Maginot Line [1] came along.

Now, I find that the home front is always having to make do with the poorest of the left-overs. For instance, I will point out to you something: all humanity has to use plumbing constantly. No scientist has ever been asked to study plumbing. Now I have to say that that is an amazing matter. To think of the extraordinary chemistries that are involved in it ... the fact that we still use four or six gallons to get rid of a pint of liquid—that kind of nonsense. This wet plumbing is where disease proliferates in the most important kinds of ways. But enough of that.

Luckily I came out of my naval service in the new world of the aeroplane and the radio and very advanced technology in general, into the building world and I did succeed in getting up 240 buildings in the early twenties and discovered that the building of a house is thousands of years behind the art of designing a ship for the sea, a ship for the sky. So I said what would happen if the little individuals were to take the most advanced technologies themselves and were to apply them to the home front where you are continually learning to do more with less? I said, what this really means —being able to do so much with so little—is that we might be able ultimately to take care of everybody.

Now, in 1927 when I undertook to do this, the American Institute of Architects had given a prize to a house in Chicago, which they called the most satisfactory single-family house for two parents and four children. I estimated its total weight, including all its equipment, and the house itself, and all the pipes to the mains and it amounted to 150 tons. Then I undertook to take the most advanced air-craft technology, because I was also skilled in that branch of engineering, and apply it to providing an equal amount of environmental control, the same volume of space and all the same services. And I made it safer still: it was earthquake-proof, and the Chicago house was not. At any rate, I came out with a total of only three tons. This told me then that this was a very extraordinary field to operate in. As I said, that was fifty years ago.

The question was: how could a little individual get on? I was penniless at the time, with a new-born child and a beautiful wife; and our first child had died five years earlier, just before its fourth birthday, so being entrusted with this

1 The Maginot Line—named after a French politician, André Maginot (1877–1932), Minister of War from 1929 to 1930, and subsequently in 1931, who had it built— was a system of defensive fortifications on France's eastern border with Germany. That 'shield' appeared to render France invulnerable in the event of overland invasion.

new life was enough to force me to make this kind of critical decision. Anyway, I realized then that nature is trying very hard to make man a success but the big function of human beings seems to be related to our being given minds able to discover principles ... that is, the small family of generalized principles found in physics: the principle of leverage, or the principle of the refraction of light. Dealing with these general principles, I came to believe that human beings apparently are given access to part of the great design of the universe itself, that we apparently are here for local monitoring and to be able to develop instrumentation to get the information gathered—local information-gatherers, as it were, and local solvers of problems common to all lives, to all history problems.

I said to myself that if human beings have been designed to be local information-gatherers and problem-solvers, it is necessary then to keep them alive; and this whole ecology is related to furthering the greater pattern of the universe itself, wherein physics has shown that there is no energy created, no energy lost but the universe itself eternally regenerative, we are part of that regenerative system. I thought if I were to commit myself to what nature seemed to be trying to do—employing this information and trying to make a man a success by developing environmental controls, homes, support of life, doing more with less, using the highest technology—perhaps nature might support my efforts and possibly make man himself a physical success. I might be able to go so far as to prove invalid the whole working assumption that it has to be you *or* me because there is not enough for both of us, which is the way we rationalize self-ishness. That was fifty years ago and since that time I have gone into a great deal of experimental development in environmental control. There are now well over a hundred thousand of my geodesic [2] structures around the world and they are in the most remote, most difficult places—there is one at the top of Mount Fuji, one over the South Pole, known as the Project Deep Freeze, and yet they have been air-delivered: they can do so much with so little, so I really know what I am talking about logistically.

Furthermore, I know a great deal about energy. When I got into environmental control I found that there was a law of design pertaining to ships which was that every time you doubled the length of a ship, you had eight times as much volume and only four times as much surface. Every time you doubled the length of a ship, you had eight times as much payload with only four times as much surface friction to drive through the sea. So, it pays to build a bigger and bigger ship.

2 Geodesic dome: strong, lightweight dome built on a framework of triangular shaped blocks. It has no internal support.

I found that every time I doubled the dimension of a geodesic dome, I had eight times as much atmosphere inside, molecules of atmosphere, but only four times as much surface. Every time I doubled, I halved the amount of surface through which an interior molecule of atmosphere could gain or lose heat; the energy efficiency went up very, very rapidly with size increase. I came to designing a theoretic geodesic dome just two miles in diameter; I actually carried out the designing of all the parts and went into all the logistics and I wanted to see what it looked like. New York's Manhattan Island is just two miles wide at 42nd Street, so I bought an aerial photograph of New York and I super-imposed my two-mile-diameter hemisphere. I found that the buildings standing below my dome were eighty-four times the surface of the dome itself. The dome was so large, the energy conservation so high, that its sun-energy empow-erment and the wind resistance of a building combined to produce so enormous a drag that air turbines driven by that drag and sun power could completely run New York City without any further energy supplied from outside.

When I look back at these studies, I am struck by the potentials that are really there for us. Yet, in our overall economy in the United States right now, we are wasting energy because of bad design. The reciprocating engine is only 15 per cent efficient, with the piston sending energy this way and the crank shaft completely contradicting this and sending it the other way. You have 15 per cent efficiency for the reciprocating engine and 30 per cent for the turbine. With the jet engine, which has no connecting rod, we get up to 60 per cent, while the fuel cells of the space programme are 85 per cent efficient. Another example: at every moment in the United States, twenty-four hours a day, some 2 million cars are standing in front of red lights with their engines running. The overall picture is so bad that out of every hundred barrels of fuel consumed we are getting only 5 per cent of work; 95 per cent is lost by absolutely bad design and management.

Now what this all brings me down to is what I have concluded is the fallacy that the resources of our earth are disappearing. We are also very ignorant about these resources. The Club of Rome [3] tends to assume, for instance, that metals are consumed like fruit and vegetables. The fact that mines are getting relatively exhausted—little metal in the mines—is absolutely irrelevant because the metals con-tinually recirculate. They are imperishable and out of all the copper mines in the whole history of man, 84 per cent of the copper is still in recirculation and we know where the other

3 In April 1968, a group of thirty scientists, economists, teachers, industrialists and national and international civil servants met at the Academia dei Lincei in Rome at the instance of Aurelio Peccei, the indus-trialist and economist, to discuss the world problems of the near future.

The proceedings of the Club of Rome, backed by the research of a team from the Massachusetts Institute of Technology (MIT), gave rise in 1972 to the publication of the first report, *The Limits to Growth*.

16 per cent is: in munition ships at the bottom of the ocean—eventually it too will come into recirculation.

For instance, in the development of the telephone, at first one given cross-section of copper transmitted a single message. Then we got to two messages on the same cross-section, and this increased to twelve, then to twenty-eight, then to 200 and ultimately to more than 2,000. By 1930 the Chief Engineer of the Bell System said that the telephone service which was then serving 10 per cent of humanity could be extended to all of humanity, without need for the telephone companies to mine or buy another pound of copper because they continually learned to do so much more with so much less. We are now at a point where one communication satellite weighing one-quarter of a ton is out-performing the transoceanic communication capabilities of 175,000 tons of copper cable. Well, by multiplying 175,000 by four, you will get an idea of the increase in the amazing possibilities of doing more with less. All the metals eventually are recovered from where they are being used, as some piece of equipment becomes obsolete or a building becomes obsolete. They do so at very different rates, but on an average all metals are recovered every twenty-two years, and every time twenty-two years comes around man's know-how has been increased so very greatly that it continually takes care of many, many more people with much higher standards of living.

Well, I found that this was not understood at all by the Club of Rome. I must therefore say certain things about total resources and the total logistics and total energy requirements, etc. I have gone a great deal into studies of the uses of small environment controls by the individual, starting fifty years ago with an attempt to make an energy-harvesting device, a sun cell and an air machine using the very powerful low drag on the tail of a building to pull air through a turbine. Using every way I could, everything I had learned in chemistry, including how to re-use human waste, I came to know a very great deal about the world's energy sources. I have been studying the total earth for a long time and my conclusions have now been published as a world planning game. That is like the old game called Battle: how do you control the great lines of supply? My world game is how to look at total resources, total humanity, how by good design to use these properly, how to be able to take care of all of humanity. And this world game, three years ago, was published in a book called *Energy, Earth and Everyone*, and in which it is spelled out absolutely clearly and simply as a design project. It is what you call a critical

path study with all the things you have to do first and how
they overlap with the next things. In the book *Energy,
Earth and Everyone*, it becomes incontrovertible that—by
using only proven energy resources, only proven technologies for employing those resources, only proven rates
which that technology can produce and put into place—
within ten years, we could have all humanity enjoying the
higher energy income that was enjoyed exclusively by North
Americans in 1972, and that during these ten years we could
phase out altogether and forever all further use of fossil fuel
and atomic energy. That is, we could live entirely on our
energy income, which is not being investigated. But it is
now incontestable that this can be done. The same thing is
possible with food. It is perfectly clear we can take care of
feeding all humanity in an absolutely competent manner
with a very large amount left over if only we look at these
things in terms of total earth, operating the total earth to the
total advantage of all of humanity.

These things are absolutely and incontrovertibly true
in terms of environmental control, building, technology in
general, energy requirements, food, and I can easily demonstrate this. There are many people who want to look
into what I am saying and find out how I can make such
statements; there are some hundreds of thousands of young
people particularly, who have looked into them and found
that they are correct. I can now say categorically that within
ten years it would be feasible for all humanity to have a
higher standard of living than human beings have yet
experienced and this for a sustained period because we will
not be using any of nature's savings-account energies and
we will not be burning up our ship. We could do this
keeping in mind the need to take care of all the generations
to come. So once I knew this was technically feasible, I then
came to the following point: I, a tiny little man, find that we
have these options and make these statements and gradually
a larger and larger number of people are checking them and
finding that they are true, but there are 4,000 million human
beings. Ninety-nine per cent of humanity does not understand science and technology. There are 40 million engineers
and scientists on our planet. That is only 1 per cent of
humanity and the 99 per cent do not understand science and
technology, and because they do not understand, they do
not know that science has never found out anything more
important than that the universe possesses the most incredible technological potential.

The universe is endowed with an incredible technology,
with most beautiful absolute regularities and principles

which are gradually being utilized by human beings on our planet, but because 99 per cent do not understand science and do not know all that science is finding out, they think of the word 'technology' as something new an they equate it only with weapons and with machinery to make money and there is an enormous antipathy to the whole idea of machinery with technology, which means really an antipathy to the universe itself. Technology is not understood and it becomes a serious matter, and I found that the reason was the following: science, which very properly requires experimental evidence to alter its position on anything, is employing mathematical tools that have no experimental evidence whatsoever. This is not the results of a conspiracy today or possibly ever; on the other hand, there may at some time have been a conspiracy, perhaps of the navigator priests 15,000 years ago, who were able to enjoy very great power by virtue of their mathematical ability. At any rate, it is perfectly preposterous when you think about it, when we say to little children: come to school now. I am not going to teach you something complicated; I am going to give you some nice simple plane geometry. When you explain to a little child what plane geometry is, you say it has two dimensions. But there is no experimental evidence of two dimensions. A surface has to be a surface of something: nothing does not have a surface. For that matter, there is no experimental evidence of the square root of —1. We find that science is still operating on X, Y, Z co-ordinates, perpendicular parallels, which were very appropriate when the earth was thought to be flat and all the perpendiculars were parallel to one another. That is not the case and the universe is operating convergently/divergently; radiation coming apart, gravitation coming together. There are no parallels in it. I found that out as a really quite young child when I became aware that I was being taught mathematics which did not have experimental evidence. I was told that a point had no dimension, that a line had one dimension, a plane two dimensions and they told me that a cube existed with three dimensions. I then said: how old is it and what is its weight and what is its temperature? It did not have any of those qualities and I was not convinced that it existed.

I began really to question things but I also learned how you could give the answers that satisfy the teacher and let you get through school all right. I was looking at the wake of a ship when I was really quite young. It was all white. And I said that is white, different from the rest of the colours —the green and the blue water there—because it is bubbles.

So, how many bubbles am I looking at on that white path
out there? Obviously an incredible number of bubbles and
each one of those bubbles I said is a sphere. I had been
taught at school that in order to design a sphere, I had to
use π. I had also been taught that π is a transcendental
irrational, can never be resolved. So, every time nature
makes one of those bubbles, how many places does she carry
out π to before she discovers that it cannot be resolved, and
at what point does nature decide to make a fake bubble?
I said I am confident nature is not using π. She is not using
any irrationals whatsoever. She is doing beautiful things,
making beautiful associations using whole numbers. So I
said that I think I am going to try to find nature's co-
ordinate system. So, starting way, way back, about seventy
years ago, I tried to find nature's co-ordinate system, and
now I am absolutely confident that I have found it and that
the co-ordinate system is all conceptual, is four-dimensional,
beautiful and always clearly demonstrable. It is arrived at
entirely by starting with reality and multiplying by the
division of demonstrable realities and there is no question
about it, it is very highly teachable. And I am now at a point
where it has now become really incontrovertible that this is
nature's co-ordinate system and it is so conceptual that little
children are going to be able to understand nuclear affairs
and understand exactly how nature makes all of her structures, associations and transformations.

This would mean then that the 99 per cent of humanity
that does not understand technology would be able to
understand technology and understand then how we can
get on with our universe, so this became the most important
news and the most important responsibility I have ever had,
and it is very important for me to let you know it. But you
have little time to devote to me to learn what I am talking
about. ... Cynergetics (nature's co-ordinate geometry) is
very big in the universities and my books concerning it are
selling in a very big way and I now know that there is a chance
for a breakthrough. We can manage to understand what
nature's evolution is about.

I would like then to make a quick little jump because I
have been at long-distance prognostications for a very long
time, give you a little idea of some of the kind of controls I
use in making long-distance prognostications. For instance,
I wondered fifty years ago if I could get some idea of the rate
of science growth versus time, and I saw that if you tried to
think about all the events of science as open-ended, there was
a close family of events as, for example, in the chemical
elements and their beautiful sequence up to uranium 92

where you have to have (it is like a serial pair of keys for getting into that club) one proton with one electron, etc., with no redundancies whatsoever. So I said, I would like to take the history of the isolation of chemical elements by human beings and study the rate at which they were able to isolate them.

History opens: we have already discovered nine chemical elements. Then in A.D. 1200 we had our first isolation of a chemical element which was arsenic, then there was a 200-year jump and we came to antimony, and then a 200-year jump to phosphorous and then suddenly after seventy-five years this curve climbs very rapidly. I then had a curve of what I call pure science against time. I have said that out of this, against this pure science background, human beings were gaining knowledge and were able to cope with various environments. They were able to cope with environments they had not been able to cope with before, so suddenly they could live where previously it had been too cold, where they would have frozen to death. It was this control that made it possible for them to exist under conditions under which they had never been able to exist before, and from inside their environmental control, to be able to control energies outside the environmental control with which they would then make a complete circuit of our earth.

Magellan [4] in a wooden sailing ship developed this environmental control to go around the Horn and from inside that environmental control, was able to put the sail on the ship and use the outside energies of the wind to take it on a complete circuit of the earth.

Three hundred and fifty years later, man went around the earth in a steel steamship. Seventy-five years later, he went around it in an aluminium aeroplane and thirty-five years later, he went around it in a rocket make of exotic metals. At the time of Magellan's ship, nobody would have dreamed a steel steamship possible; at the time of the steel steamship, nobody would have dreamed that we would have an aluminium aeroplane and at the time of the aluminium aeroplane, nobody dreamed we would have rockets of exotic metals. Each was completely uncontemplated by the previous state of the art.

The wooden sailing ship took two years to make a circuit; the steel steamship took two months, the aeroplane took two weeks to do it the first time, and the exotic-metals rocket, a little over one hour. We have here a basic acceleration in time of the isolation of chemical elements by the scientists, similarly, there is this 350-, 75-, 35-year contraction between each new state of the art, and then

4 Ferdinand Magellan (1480–1521), the Portuguese navigator, wished to find a passage to the Moluccas and Asia round the south of America. With the support of the Emperor Charles V he was able to prepare the expedition and left Spain in 1519 with five vessels. He passed through the straits now named after him and reached the Philippines, where he was killed in a local skirmish. Circumnavigation took three years and two weeks.

the rate at which they went around the earth also contracting.[5] This is a four- or rather a three-dimensional acceleration of energy events. Put all this on a chart covering 800 years and it is absolutely clear that by 1985, we are going to do something equally exciting as the things that were done between the aluminium aeroplane and the exotic-metals rocket. And implicit on that chart is something as unpredicted as going round the world by radio. I want all of you to feel the acceleration of these events; it is enormous. So, I would say that if we make it, if we do stay on our planet, and I think it is absolutely touch-and-go whether we do—if we are here in the twenty-first century, we will be way beyond the great crisis, and if we are here in any great numbers, as compared to today, the word 'nation' will be a word you look up in the dictionary and such phrases as 'earning a living' will be absolutely preposterous with no meaning whatsoever. It is absolutely clear that we could take care of all humanity at the highest standard of living anybody has ever known—that could have been done long, long ago. We will have stopped altogether equating eating and earning a living with money, with work. We will have human beings completely freed to do what they really always wanted to do from childhood onwards. Man wants to demonstrate competence. We would have humanity really co-operating because it understood things.

This brings me back to technology and the lack of understanding by people as a whole. Take, for instance, a sailor who goes to sea in a sailing ship. Not only does he soon know all the ropes but he begins to know everything about that ship in great detail and he knows all the human beings on board and everything they can do and how well they can do it. When it comes to a crisis on a sailing ship, you do not need any politician to tell you what to do: everybody co-operates absolutely spontaneously because they all know what it is all about. The only time you are going to get humanity co-operating spontaneously, which we would all like to have it do, will be when humanity knows what it is all about.

And I would like to point out that we are in an incredible predicament today because of too much specialization on our planet. At some time in history, we unquestionably had a man born bigger than other men like a stallion born bigger than another stallion. When that happens there is a king stallion and he fights the young one to see which one will inseminate the herd. Unquestionably, every once in a while a man was born very much bigger than the others but that was long, long ago. But the little people said: 'Please Mister,

5 It seems to have been during the Renaissance that the notion of acceleration was first put into figures. In *Civitas Solis* (1623), describing a philosophical republic, Tommaso Campanella, the person relating his discussions with the inhabitants of the City of the Sun, writes: 'They say that in our days more events worthy of history take place in a hundred years than occurred in the 4,000 years before, and that in the last century more books have been published than in the previous fifty centuries.' (On Tommaso Campanella's Utopia, see also the article by Tchavdar Kuranov on page 130.)

reach me one of those things, I can't reach', and they said: 'You're big, you get up and protect us when the enemy is trying to come at us here.' And the big man found himself being exploited for his size and he found himself having to fight all the time protecting people who were trying to come in and take the life-support from his tribe. So he said: 'I have to control things between these battles.' And they said: 'All right, we will make you king.' We then have the big man learning instinctively—if you *are* the power, the power structure—'Don't let two big men come at me at once. We'll have to divide to conquer. We'll also have to keep conquered, keep divided'. And the big man, the king, then found the two big men coming, one big man at a time. He said: 'I'm not going to kill you because I need you to do battle with me when we're being attacked, but I'm going to keep you two big men far apart. I'm going to spy on you and watch you all the time so you don't gang up on me.' Also then very many little people began to bother the power structure. The little people were not following their ruler and were brought in one by one and were told: 'We're going to cut your head off because you are a nuisance around here.' And the little man said to the king: 'Mr King, you'd better not cut my head off because I understand the language of your enemy over the hill and you don't. I heard him say what he is going to do to you and when he's going to do it.' So the king said: 'All right, that's a pretty good idea: you tell me all of what my enemy is saying over the hill and you are going to do something you've never done before: eat regularly—right up here at the castle.' One by one, various individuals who were making trouble for the power structure also demonstrated some very special capability in order to follow their instinct of divide to conquer and keep conquered, keep divided.

The power structure makes all of the specialists. So finally we have a king with a very powerful country and he has a man who has all the spy news and somebody who is very good at metallurgy, making better swords; and somebody else who is better at arithmetic and someone else is better at logistics. Finally, the king wants to hand on his kingdom to his son and he says to his specialists: 'I see you're getting very old: you, No. 1, teach somebody about that metallurgy, and I want you, No. 3, to teach somebody about that arithmetic.' This, in a way, is how a university such as Oxford is founded. [6] The way the power structure copes with the bright ones is to make them all specialists.

Now fifteen years ago, the American Association for the Advancement of Science [7] held its annual congress.

6 Oxford University, which dates back to 1133, is made up of a group of private foundations (the colleges) each of which originally tended to specialize in a particular branch of learning.

7 The American Association for the Advancement of Science is the best-known of all American scientific associations. Founded in 1848 in Washington, it has 125,000 members and publishes the review *Science*.

There were two research teams with very independent paths present at that congress—one in anthropology and the other in biology. The team of anthropologists had for some years been studying all known case-histories of human tribes that had become extinct, looking for something in common. The biology group for a number of years had been studying all the known biological species that had become extinct, looking for something in common. They were completely independent of one another. These two teams discovered independently that extinction is a consequence of over-specialization, that in nature we can in-breed special capability and as you inbreed, you outbreed general adaptability. For instance, we have a type of bird that feeds on marine life in seaside marshes and we have the Ice Age coming, so the waters are receding in the marshes by the sea. Only the long-beaked birds can reach their food and the short-beaked birds die off. So that when only the long-beak procreates, there is a concentration on the genes of the long-beaks. They get on very well so far as we have seen. But suddenly there is a marsh fire and it is discovered for the first time that beaks have become so big, they cannot fly any longer. That is what I mean by loss of general adaptability. Similarly, humanity is at a very extraordinary moment today where we are so specialized that all the specialists leave it to somebody else to make things work and I have heard a great deal about the scientists who are seemingly highly responsible but who allowed things to go wrong. I find the scientist has absolutely no authority over socio-economic affairs. The scientist's economic boss tells him: 'Now don't get involved with applied science; that's very poor, low-order stuff. You stay a beautiful pure scientist and see if you can get a Nobel Prize. You just lay eggs and we'll decide what to do with them.' We find then that the power structure simply leaves no latitude to the specialists whatsoever. So the scientists really have nothing to do with what is going on in our predicament today even though as human beings they would like very much to be able to do something about it.

Now, this is my main theme: I want to see a society which is comprehensively aware of what it is about, like the sailors on the sailing ship. Specialization is working completely against that as well as the lack of knowledge of the 99 per cent of what science and technology are all about and what our options really are.

I have introduced you to several things you may be unfamiliar with, such as lightweight structures and my kind of technology and my approach to mathematics, and time will simply have to make it clear to you that those things do exist.

I am very confident they do. Everything we meet then, as I see it, is touch-and-go and I am having a very extraordinary experience because more and more the young are learning that, as I say, there are some options. They come around to check up. And they read my books more and more and, for the last year, I have averaged an audience of 2,000 every four days and in all kinds of places where I would never have expected any audience at all. I am amazed by how many people know these things and trust me. I talk and find these great audiences are discovering we do have options. The western United States is just a little more cross-bred than the eastern and there is a young cross-breeding world here and this young world is coming through in a very extraordinary kind of way. First, in the sixties it decided that it was going to do its own thinking. It decided that it was perfectly clear that Mum and Dad did not have anything to do with going to the moon and did not have to do with anything else and the world was in trouble and if they were going to get anywhere, they were going to have to do their own thinking.

I do not want to repeat myself,[8] but in this young world I find each child is being born in the presence of less misinformation and of a much larger inventory of reliable information and each child is completely innocent of the misconditioned reflexes of the elders. They are thus able to cope with the new information in a much more effective manner. I am getting a great deal of mail and I now get letters in increasing numbers from children who were born after man got to the moon and these children have discovered that there was someone like myself that they could write to about their concerns. To them it is perfectly clear that human beings can really make this earth work. And they say: 'Why aren't we doing it?' I can see a young world coming soon, intent upon making it work. This is the best news I have but I say whether we are going to make it or not, is very, very touch-and-go and dependent on all the conditioned reflexes and the kind of things we find it really necessary to talk about.

8 The author is alluding to the remarks he made at the Round Table on Cultural and Intellectual Co-operation and the New International Economic Order, held by Unesco in Paris from 23 to 25 June 1976. He said in particular: 'Humanity is going through its final examination. If it comes out of the group womb with mind in control, we will make it.' See p. 164 of *Cultures*, Vol. III, No. 4, 1976—an issue entirely devoted to the Round Table.

We can turn the tide

Michel Jobert

It is refreshing to be gathered here today bringing with us
as we do the sum of our experience and the broad spectrum
of ideas that each of us stands for. The spectrum I mean
is not that of our different political colours, but our experience in politics, history, culture and art. I do not think any
of us has ever felt that our discussions over the next few
days might be fundamental in fashioning the evolution of
humanity. And as I sit here listening, I realize how readily
we intellectuals—which we around this table all are—take
refuge in the comforting sanctuary of concepts.

I recognize the familiar process of observing how
intellectuals feel they have achieved a great deal by setting
out a procedure for logical reasoning and arriving at a fairly
clear-cut definition of their aims, regardless of how imprac-
ticable they may be.

There is a great deal of talk today about a new world or
international economic order. This is indeed a noble
pursuit if we direct our efforts along those lines, but it is a
concept, and to my mind as unrealistic in the world of today
—let us face the facts—as when in France, my own country,
they talk to us about a 'new society', or a 'project for
society': they are merely words.

Politicians in particular, when they can fall back on
general concepts, feel better for a few hours or a few years,
thinking they have made a contribution, if not to the progress of humanity, at least to its stability and survival.

And so I am rather sceptical when we talk about the
challenges of the year 2000. The idea of these 'challenges'
has only come to the fore quite recently—it is a very fashion-

able term. Not that it is a bad thing for us all to be agreed on an up-to-date terminology, but to my mind there are not a thousand and one different challenges, especially as regards the future of our world. If we must use the word, I would suggest that there is only one challenge, and that is our *will* to do something. There is a line of Paul Valéry's —a French author often quoted when a subject combines politics and philosophy—which goes: 'Le vent se lève, il faut tenter de vivre' —the wind is rising, we must try to live.[1]

And that, today, more than at any other time in history, is the crux of the matter: to try to live. Trying to live cannot be achieved by making speeches, but by positive action, however insignificant, by our own daily determination and not simply that of our governments, on to whom responsibility is so readily shifted, that is to say, responsibility for being what we are but do not dare to be. That is the true meaning of the transfer of responsibilities. But governments cannot lay down how individuals must think. It is the individuals who, acting as freely as their status of mature, thinking human beings will allow, create the conditions for awareness, not with a view to defining goals, but in terms of positive daily action. It has been said that there has always been a discrepancy between aims and means; I myself would say that aims are always doubtful. Are they even sincere? But on the other hand, we have the means available: all the reports we have had on the progress of humanity over the past two decades are enlightening. We always have the means to act, provided that we have the will to do so, and that this will is geared to the prospect of survival.

What matters is the determination to act, as individuals, as members of a community, however small or great, as regions or as nations.

The most useful thing we can do, although I do not know whether we shall succeed in doing it, is to explore the real poles of power and influence. I have been very interested to hear about the progress made by humanity, and the dangers inherent in that progress, over the past twenty-five years. But it seemed to me that the analysis was incomplete, and that when listing the facts, we should at least also have been seeking out their underlying causes. If you had gone back thirty years or slightly more, it would have included the Yalta agreements,[2] and we should have had a picture of the world today, not as it is in theory, but an overall picture of what it has been, in its somewhat fossilized state, over the past thirty years. We must proceed from the actual situation as it stands; humanity is a living entity, not a conservatory. And consequently, if we want to take stock of the dangers

1   *Le Cimetière Marin* (1920).

2   From 4 to 11 February, 1945, Roosevelt, Churchill and Stalin met at the Crimean port of Yalta (U.S.S.R.) to discuss the peace settlement.

ahead, we must look back on how we have progressed since
1945.

The truth is, we have hardly progressed politically. The
world was divided more or less conspicuously between two
great empires. And that is still the situation today. In my
humble opinion, we cannot possibly understand anything
that goes on in the world unless we bear this in mind. What
about Bandung,[3] you may say, or the emergence of the
Third World, or the throbbing restlessness which has laid
hold on many of the peoples of the world, not as States, but
deep down as nations? These are indeed to be counted to
the credit of the last twenty years, but the fact remains that—
apart from this outward spirit of protest, from this well-
contained, well-controlled action by the Third World
countries—we are still as we were after Yalta.

What we must realize is that this situation, which is ours
today, did not simply happen; it is the result of the great
upheaval of 1939–45, and today, of all the worthwhile,
important steps we intellectuals or politicians can take, there
is one that is crucial—what we have to do is to challenge
great empires of any kind, to challenge overbearing doctrines,
at all times. Anyone who has any part in the shaping of
history or who has any insight into historical analysis knows
that great empires, and doctrines, always end up in violence
perpetrated by the State to the detriment of the individual.

Challenging great empires does not mean waging war on
them or driving them to the point of triggering off a nuclear
war (which would not be at their own expense, of course,
but at the expense of others). It simply means having the
will to say no, firmly. It is not a very difficult thing to ask:
the countries of Europe could do it today if they had the
least desire to do so, through their leaders or even their
peoples. The European countries could quietly tell the great
empires which have divided the world between them that
Europe is a power to be reckoned with. I am not saying this
because I am European or for the pleasure of setting a
medium-sized star in the world firmament, but because I do
not think the world's future lies in these great power blocs.
The right future for us is in the sharing of power among as
many as possible. (Mrs Han Suyin will forgive me, I trust,
for picking up the word 'many'.)[4] If Europe is of interest
to the world today, that interest has nothing to do with
trading with such-and-such a country, or with having been
witness to a grand and often difficult history: the point of
the interest taken in Europe is that it should not delay too
long in showing isolated peoples, or such groups as may be
formed among peoples, that there is a quiet way of chal-

3 In May 1955, the Conference of Afro-Asian Nations
was convened in Bandung
(Java) by India, Pakistan,
Ceylon, Burma and Indonesia.
It brought together representatives of thirty Asian and
African countries, most of
them independent since 1945.
The conference accepted the
principle of grants from the
Great Powers to solve the
problems of underdevelop-
ment, and condemned
racialism and colonialism.

4 An allusion to her novel
A Many-splendoured Thing.

lenging power and demanding that it be shared. That would be the great opportunity to be seized in the years to come, and I hope it will be a reality by the year 2000!

For if we remain hidebound in our present-day pattern —a pattern of imbalance caused by dominant interests— the consequences for the greater part of mankind can only be a trail of crises, constraints and, at any rate, the reverse of progress. Sharing power, on which much might be said, to judge by current trends, means first of all sharing technology and sharing monetary and commercial responsibility. How can we hope to deal comprehensively with the rosy or frightening prospects for the year 2000 if we do not face the fundamental fact that most of the world today is dependent on a single national currency?

Speaking as a member of a nation which is neither big nor small, and which consequently cannot be classed as average, I would argue that it is not possible to speak of 'consensus' —since that is the fashionable word (again, a concept)— or of world balance, as long as the strings, especially the monetary strings, are all pulled one way, to serve the interests of one power. That, today, is the most urgent issue on which we must ask for a sharing of power, and if possible, achieve it. So that 85 per cent of the International Monetary Fund,[5] for example, will no longer be controlled by a single power. Indeed, I have no objection to a re-examination of the role of my own country in the Monetary Fund; my argument goes far deeper than the defence of national interests, which is, in any case, short-sighted. What I want to say, as clearly and as firmly as I can, is that we are courting disaster by relying on the cool-headed vision the United States has of its own position as a supreme power.

But where is this leading us, I ask? There has been much talk of the European Parliament to be elected by universal suffrage, and of the Common Market, which has been neatly broken up by all sorts of monetary arrangements and quotas. In point of fact, we are heading for a revival of customs restrictions; it has already begun in some countries, and Japan's brilliant trade offensive brings the prospect even

5 The International Monetary Fund was founded in Washington on 27 December 1945 following the United Nations Monetary and Financial Conference (Bretton Woods, 1–22 July 1944). Its aims were to promote international monetary co-operation for the expansion of international trade.

nearer. And therefore what we must all set our minds on, using our own common sense, our goodwill, our relentless will to succeed, is a world where justice reigns. There is no justice, either, in our present world, as far as armaments are concerned. I do not know whether we shall succeed, after all the statements and conferences on the subject—and which, if you will allow me to say so, are all completely hypocritical—I do not know whether we shall succeed in easing the terrifying military pressures that are a permanent threat to our planet.

How can we do so? Having spoken of the will to act, I should now like to speak about the citizen's responsibility. In the final analysis, the world cannot be worthy of that name if there is no individual consciousness, and by that I do not mean the individual for the individual, out of sheer egotism. I believe that what we must aim at is the 'individual in society', a person who thinks of himself or herself as being part of a corporate group. Our most hopeful prospect for the next twenty years is that among the peoples of the world, at whatever stage of development they may be, the concept of the free choice of the individual within the community and for the community should gather momentum. A system could very well be devised, provided that the will is there, and provided that power structures are broken down and re-defined to provide scope for the individual to flourish. Looking at political and social life in my own country, I would say that we have not yet reached that stage. In France, the individual has only the freedom to choose which badge he will pin on his lapel and then, by casting a vote, to hand over to others the right to think out and organize the life of the community. I myself believe in step-by-step, day-by-day progress by individuals. It is up to them to organize their own lives, and in order to achieve this, to break loose from those doctrines which, as I said just now, always lead to violence inflicted on them by the State or by vested interests. I have in mind here liberal as well as Marxist doctrines. We all have a right to an area of freedom; and within that area of freedom we must assume our respon-sibilities. We talk so much about democracy: look where democracy is in the world! It is a relic, a fragile, threatened plant—worse still, it is often pure caricature! It is nineteenth-century democracy, in which the citizen, who knows his place and is well-versed in the requirements of the democratic order, delegates his powers from vote to vote, or in other words plays a purely passive role, and in most countries hides behind a little curtain when expressing his opinion. Surely, in the twentieth century, the time has come to move on to a twentieth-century democracy, which as we know cannot be a repetition of the nineteenth-century version.

This 'English model' of democracy has failed in most countries where it does not meet the underlying desires of the 'individual in society' who has suddenly emerged as a responsible being, much more rapidly than we did in the West, where the process took much longer.

At this point, I should like to say a word about culture. Culture is not the prefabricated fare we are fed every day by the vast, too-conventional network of media for the dissemination of thought. Culture, in my view, is already represented by the malaise that has taken hold of so many individuals adrift in a sick world. They are anxious, they search their hearts to find out more about themselves and about what they hear and see. And for that reason we must never, I think, lose faith in culture, not the culture that is encased in film-reels, photographs or books, but the whole culture that springs from a non-conventional uneasiness in the individual.... From an uneasiness that eludes impassive, overbearing doctrines, set patterns and State dogma, and I would even go as far as to say, social conventions. You will realize that the point I wish to make here is the importance of diversity. It is one of the most imperative contributions we have to make. All the uniformity that our technological civilization has inflicted on our lives, not only on us who live in the West, but also in the East, in Africa, South America and elsewhere—that uniformity is everywhere and always a crime against history. Why? Because it cuts us off from our historical roots, and asks us to forget them and behave in a way that is convenient for the smooth running of economic life, the great flow of international trade. But for whom? And for what? That is a fundamental question, to be asked with some concern.

The form of diversity I have been speaking about is cultural, but it also has a material aspect: the liberating act for the individual is not necessarily—and now I am, of course, caricaturing the situation—to wear blue jeans because that is the fashion, or to eat what other people tell you you should eat. On the contrary, the yearning we now see everywhere for a revival of traditional values, the impassioned, desperate, deeply moving struggle of individuals to rise above the cloying surface of material conformity all bespeak a spirit of cultural protest to which we must give heed and which must be defended at all costs.

As for politics, a field in which it has fallen to me from time to time, and even now, to play a modest part, there is one requirement to be met: it must not consciously be thought of as the stronghold of cynicism. Political activity is warranted only when it seeks, however clumsily, to reconcile its undertakings with ethics and with history: all unethical political acts detract from humanity. I know from my own experience that it is no easy task to take part in politics and defend the ethical viewpoint, to bring the air of morality into the political atmosphere. But our time on this earth is brief, for all of us; I do not even know if we who are today discussing the year 2000 will still be here when it comes. There must be others, younger than ourselves, who might have spoken with a greater sense of their responsibility about the turn of the century. But we must at least, by what we do, leave a token to show that we were at one point concerned about relating our political attitude to morality.

Let us see, then, how we can pay due regard to ethics in political action. Admittedly, when faced with the present popularity of somewhat abstract notions like ecology or self-management, expressed as they are in a variety of ways, we may sometimes be surprised or irritated. But there seem to me to be two underlying moral preoccupations in both these movements: in ecology, without a doubt, the notion of respect. In the first place, the immediate, obvious respect owed to oneself in relation to nature, the respect owed to others. And in the growing demand for self-management throughout the world, in the concept itself, dissociated from any political interpretation, I see only the often-captive individual's fundamental demand that he should be responsible for his own commitment to living in society and responsible, too, for putting all his imagination into the task of living in society, however tiny his share may be. It is not a question of re-writing the Ten Commandments, but simply perhaps of working out a system of garbage-collection in self-complacent countries like ours where we no longer want immigrant labour but are only too pleased to have it between 5 and 7 o'clock in the morning! But that is what the organization of community life means. That is what responsibility and imagination mean—it is as ordinary and as trivial as that. And it is through such attitudes that politics can be joined with ethics, through respect and through responsibility. But in what direction are we heading now?

Well, we know that we run a permanent risk of disaster. There are those who believe in localized conflicts, and indeed, how could they do otherwise? Look at what is happening in the Near East. My contention, although I may be wrong, is that no one can understand what is going on in the Near East without grasping the fact that there, on that perennial battleground of history, where people have built up a considerable memory of events, rancour and mystique, the explanation for the conflicts and troubles must be sought first and foremost in the attitudes of the U.S.S.R. and the United States—two great powers who by common consent have decided that it is not inconvenient for them to have a state of controlled conflict in that area. No one will be able to understand events in the Lebanon over the past few months unless they look at them in that light. Yes, of course, there are Lebanese involved, but the others are far more important and omnipresent. Without going too deeply into the subject, I would say that localized conflicts are indeed always possible. And while we are on the subject, does the Viet Nam war mean anything to you? It has only just ended, and United States policy seems to me to be still smarting under the blow of that event. And a great event it was. But tomorrow there could be other Viet Nams, somewhere else. Which is why, even though it may not necessarily contribute substantially to peace, the sharing of power will help to re-establish some sort of equilibrium in the world.

But if there are conflicts, we shall find that tomorrow we will scarcely be any better off than today, as vulnerable as ever; and in fact it is not the year 2000 that I fear but, far more, 1979 (not our national year 1978, for which I do not fear at all, as it happens!). But I am apprehensive of 1979, and 1980. Who can say at this stage whether those who govern, or think they govern, the world are capable of mastering the great economic phenomena? No science is more venerable, or more uncertain, than economics. I have spent my life admiring economists, and yet at the same time suffering in silence each time they went wrong, in other words constantly!

By 1939, Franklin Roosevelt's New Deal had worn thin. It was to be a failure. And what solution did humanity find to save itself from complete chaos and disaster, but full employment! Not with the help of Keynes,[6] but with the war. There was a perfect example of full employment: there were people in the camps, others in the army, others working in factories—everyone was busily working away all over the world. That was full employment, and who knows whether it will not be an acceptable solution to tomorrow's problems? Supposing there were a sort of bankruptcy brought about by copper, coffee and a few other commodities. I am not at all sure we would be able to prevent the system from breaking down, in the state it is at the moment. That is why I am not daunted so much by the prospect of 2000—which, for that matter, is not very far off either—as by today.

Basically, I am very optimistic about the age we live in. We are still suffering the after-effects of the Yalta partitions, and the lopsided world they created. But all around us there are people of great interest to us, people who want to live: there is the Third World, and there is the Fourth World which, heaven knows, has difficulty in existing at all! And even in our Western and Eastern countries, under different regimes, people are managing to give voice, sometimes in the face of great odds, to a sort of collective awareness quite

6 John Maynard Keynes (1883–1946). English economist and mathematician whose unorthodox economic theories at the beginning of this century (in 1919, Keynes attacked the economic arrangements of the Treaty of Versailles) were to have a long and lasting influence on the policies of the developed countries, particularly as regards employment. The New Deal was directly inspired by Keynes' theories; Keynes had, in fact, advocated a policy of public expenditure to the extent of incurring budgetary deficit in order to absorb unemployment. The idea of spending more to regain prosperity was very startling at the time.

distinct from the official patterns of thought, however subtly or stringently they may be put across. The growing anxiety which has taken hold on our civilizations gives me, I will not say great satisfaction, but great hope. It tells me that we must not despair of the times we live in, that we today are capable of great things if we concede that those who wield power today and who are vulnerable beings, often defence-less when they seem all-powerful, appear in that guise only for the purposes of our own obsolete conception of comfort. It is we who keep them powerful, but in fact, throughout the world, the emperor is naked. He *is* naked but we are not yet aware of it because public opinion is chary of saying out loud what it thinks of monetary problems, international trade, a more equitable sharing of world power, the use of the atom for peaceful ends or the reverse.

So far, nothing has been said openly. For it is quite certain that neither the United States nor the U.S.S.R. could go ahead with their intensive arms build-up if public opinion at home put up the least opposition to their policies on the ground that they are suicidal and must be stopped. Even if public opinion began by saying this policy is first of all fatal for others, what a boost would be given to public opinion, such as it is, in the U.S.S.R. and in the United States!

And so I wish to conclude on a note of optimism and hope. I like my own time; I am not one of those who say that children do not know how to behave, that the younger generation does not believe in anything, and that we are doomed to catastrophe. No, I believe that the future is wide open. I *do* think, as I said before, that our goals are question-able and too narrowly defined, but the means to achieve them are available and the use made of them depends on our own will, if and when that will can be expressed. The time is favourable for free will to develop, not in the eighteenth-of nineteenth-century sense of every man for himself, but in the sense of highly diversified groups united in a common purpose focused on the idea of equilibrium on a world scale. Since there has been a great deal of talk about techno-logy, I should like to suggest a ray of hope: we are obsessed by the great spectre of destruction looming over our heads, but perhaps tomorrow it will be within the power of each and every one of us to neutralize that immense arsenal, and all that trouble, all that expense will answer no further purpose. We shall find ourselves in a more familiar atmo-sphere of abated tension and then, as we shall be less com-mitted to building up armaments, we shall perhaps be able to concentrate on development.

There can be no world as we know it without human beings, but neither can there be a world without mankind as a whole: either we let nature take its implacable, always well-timed course, crushing down some and multiplying others, or we seek, in an economic system based on solidarity, in a sharing of responsibility and in a keen awareness of others (which is also self-interest) the understanding and the possibility of taking our world in hand through our own personality.

Postscript

We cite here extracts from an interview in the course of which Mr Jobert explained or tempered certain points in his speech:

We are looking ahead to the year 2000, and we are right to do so. Only a little while ago there was something almost unreal about the prospect; but suddenly it is within grasping distance, ours and our children's.

But we would be wiser to concern ourselves with the months or years that lie immediately ahead. Economic imbalances have reached such a point that the likeliest probability is that the experts will be caught off-guard: the unexpected will scotch their speculations. The world economic machine could just as unpredictably get out of control as seize up, and it would be as much of a surprise to them as it would to us, when we pick up our morning newspaper.

Up till now, economic crises have had any significant impact on us only when they deeply affected the affluent nations of the world. And yet we must all be conscious of the fact that there has been no remission in the devastation they have wrought in a world whose cries have been curiously stifled even when they were the voices of multitudes. A crisis is not a major one outside New York or London. In Calcutta, it is merely a news item.

But that time is past. The world of banking and international trade—a cosy world for some—is on its beam ends: crises can no longer be shuffled off to some forgotten, over-populated part of the globe. The notion of letting fate take its course without questioning what it is all about is no longer part of people's make-up. They can be relied on at the end of this twentieth century to seek out relentlessly what causes are at work, what responsibilities have to be borne, what mechanisms operate. We need only see with what determination the Third World governments, using every means of pressure at hand, mean to make use of the population weapon.

We have now to work for and win a world of respect—and long before the year 2000. So far it has shown scant respect for the individual, for groups of individuals, for the environment or for a moral code, so that it is not surprising that the world today has increasingly lost its respectability in the eyes of those who live in it and whose attitudes towards it have now become circumspect or angry. A world of respect is not one which upholds cynical diversions of power, indifference to the weak, or political or economic systems whose ultimate aims for man and his environment are fundamentally debatable.

Fortunately, a great many people are now at work, searching. This phenomenon can probably be attributed to modern means of information and communication, even though the use made of them is all too likely to be anything but honest. Perhaps the end of the twentieth century will mark the beginning of the free agency of man in society, combining efforts to safeguard threatened identities, a welcome intrusion of cultural diversity into the realm of politics, and the search for a multi-polar universe in which the complex web of tensions and ententes will be found preferable to armed peace manipulated by a handful of powers.

But it would be a great pity to sit here brooding over the present time which is daunting only in that is is still shackled to the weighty burden of the past. Mature thought and diligence have given us the means to turn the tide of events if it should seem suicidal. We are not helplessly facing the inevitable. No, we are now at a point where we can take the exact measure of our own wisdom and apply it to our lives.

It is likely that even more serious imbalances lie in store for this technologically orientated civilization of ours before it comes to realize that it is on the wrong track. If it is to endure, it will certainly have to undergo radical change, for which it will have to accept two ideas that have hitherto been anathema to it: the sharing of power, right down to the level of the individual and, on the other hand, that diversity which will become the only effective means human societies will have to react against 'non-entity', the fate to which the road to so-called 'progress' will ultimately lead them,

Our most pressing duty, therefore, is to rid ourselves of militant, unshakable, false ideologies that over-simplify the true issues, to give each individual scope to act freely, to seek to achieve responsibility rather than obedience, to accept the dictates of the State in a spirit of tolerance and wariness.

At each period of its history, the world has, almost unwittingly, woven its own fabric of insecurity or hope. Without waiting for the year 2000, I have faith in my own time, for it appears to me to have at last awakened to its surroundings and embarked on a relentless inventory which I feel sure holds out great hope for the future.

The danger of irreconcilable objectives

Paul-Marc Henry

The challenge of the year 2000 has been construed essentially as that confronting an organized, self-aware human community, with access to common sources of information and having at its disposal an even more highly efficient network of communications than there is today. But the reality of the present-day world brings home to us the fact that this global system does not exist in our imaginations and that, for practical purposes, the nation-States are all outlining for themselves the next twenty-five years in accordance with their own conception of society. The question we must ask ourselves, therefore, is whether these different concepts of society can be reconciled on the global scale, whether they can be applied without a major world conflict, whether, in other words, the goals that various groups of people propose to achieve are not fundamentally contradictory.

We have been told that China feels basically that war is inevitable and that once it is over, a new threshold of development will be crossed. This view has, at least, the advantage of being realistic, since it is quite conceivable that China's blueprint for society and those of, say, the Soviet Union, Japan, Europe and the United States of America, not to mention those of the developing countries, of course, may not be reconcilable with one another. Reference is made to the obvious over-consumption which would result from adoption of the Western consumption pattern on a world scale, but before looking at its cumulative, aggregate effects, we should first examine what is at present contemplated in national plans.

We have seen the results, for example, of one highly successful national plan over the past twenty-odd years, namely that of Japan. From 1950 to 1977, Japan has succeeded in maintaining a real annual growth rate of 10–15 per cent, resulting in increased consumption and production and causing some upheaval in international trade. With Japan, we have reached what I shall now term a 'critical threshold'. To take the example of the motor-car industry, for instance: the rise in production must at some point be curbed, for one cannot go on indefinitely producing 10 or 12 million more cars a year and exporting them only to those countries that can afford them.

These 'thresholds' are now becoming familiar ground. Take the textile industry in Asian countries, for instance, where very low cost, high-quality goods are manufactured. Productivity is extremely high and the machinery used very sophisticated. I do feel, therefore, that before launching out into joint planning ventures, the points of conflict and critical thresholds inherent in conflicting development projects must be analysed. It is not sure that the current growth target of the Soviet Union, with a real annual rate of 6–7 per cent, can be reconciled with a 6 per cent growth rate in Western Europe—it is not at all sure. And this is not because we have not enough natural resources, but because, owing to the interplay of market and finance structures, there are inevitable critical and contradictory points. And world conflicts occur precisely when there is a clash between conflicting views on society. Look at the 1914–18 war. Even now, with historical hindsight, we do not really know who caused it. Historians have still not made up their minds.

What can be said, however, is that Germany's economic development had reached a critical stage at that time as compared with Russia, which was still lagging behind, and as compared with British and even French development at that juncture. The United States were not yet to be reckoned with as a great economic power. And in the context of the year 2000, the problem is now this: what are the critical thresholds we are going to reach in the very near future? Indeed, we may ask, what is the North–South issue? My answer is that it is a threshold, a critical, conflict-wrought threshold of opposing interests; why deny it?

When the government of one of the affluent countries such as France, for example, restricts the import of products from poor countries (or at any rate from poorer countries with high productivity, for example in the textile industry), this raises a basic question: will those countries be able to find

1 'Could we convert more than 2,000 million marks into foreign currency each year? We could not, and yet we did, by initially borrowing the money from abroad and subsequently paying it back', writes Dr Schacht, ex-President of the Reichsbank, in his memoirs (see Note 3 below). The Dawes Plan relating to reparations laid down that the German debt was to be paid in annual instalments, gradually rising from 1,000 million to 2,000 million gold marks. It was effective from August 1924 to May 1930 (when it was superseded by the Young Plan), during which period 7,170 million gold marks were paid out, partly in services.

2 The Young Plan (named after the American expert, Owen D. Young), provided for the German debt to be paid in fifty-nine annual instalments (payable up to 1988) and established a *de facto* link between the German and the allied debts. (Because of the 1931 financial crisis, it was never carried out.) It set up the Bank for International Settlements, with its headquarters in Basle.

3 'Germany was an industrialized country which had still further improved its industrial build-up since the war.... The economic history of the last few decades made it clear that loans had to be granted in the first place to the less-developed countries, to help them develop their raw materials and step up the process of industrialization. It was pointless to force Germany, as had been done previously, to compete with the other European industrialized countries. Competition had been one of the major causes of the 1914–18 war and was to be avoided. Peaceful arrangements could be promoted by opening up a

markets in solvent, wealthy economies, or will they be debarred from them?

I should like, in this connection, to remind you of two interesting figures with regard to the much-discussed question of international debts (and which in my opinion illustrate to perfection a fundamental critical point). The figures are these: the developing, non-oil-producing countries have accrued a short- and medium-term debt of approximately $200,000 million, according to International Monetary Fund statistics.

The Soviet Union and the socialist countries are fast nearing the $50,000 million mark, on a more or less short-term basis. This means that, between these countries and the developing countries, there is an outstanding debt of at least $250,000 million owed to the West.

And how are these debts to be repaid, except by one of the following two means. They could be written off. But that is out of the question, for it would create havoc in all our systems of credit. Another way of writing them off is to let them dwindle through inflation. The alternative is to repay them in goods and services.

Now that was precisely the dilemma that had to be faced in 1929–30 in the case of Germany,[1] which could pay reparations only by exporting its industrial production; but at that time, Dr Schacht, who was then President of the Reichsbank, pointed out to Mr Young, the author of the Young Plan[2] which you may recall, that the only way for the Germans to pay their debts was to pour their surplus production into the Third World countries—then known as overseas countries.[3] It is my belief that the situation we are in today is exactly comparable.

We have, on the one hand, a colossal debt, steadily increasing (at a rate of about 10 per cent per annum) owed by the developing and East European countries, each of which, incidentally, creates different production potentials, and on the other, our basic need to export to those countries. But our markets are saturated. As we have already said, we cannot have four refrigerators each, or five colour television sets each. Our markets are glutted and this was the very argument we brought out in 1929 against having German reparations paid in kind, at the time when payment was being demanded in gold. But we cannot possibly expect the developing countries to pay us in gold, even if the Soviet Union might perhaps be asked to do so. We have, in fact, arrived at a 'critical threshold'.

This is where I think technological projections come into their own. The year 1929 was excellent for technological projections: television and telecommunications were then just around the corner, and the 1929–30 technological revolution was, on a smaller scale, comparable to ours. But we are now at a critical threshold, as we were in 1929, on a much larger scale.

And so it seems to me that, before we start talking about the year 2000, every nation which still exercises its own options should question its own future in terms of the year 2000. Which means that each nation should ask itself: what will become of our children, how will they be employed, what will our national production consist of, what will our standard of living be like? And this brings us back to the question already raised: if each country defines its own rate of consumtion for the next twenty-five years, it must take some decisions here and now. And when we talk of placing ceilings or an overall curb on the global, combined consumption of the West, we seem to be assuming that there is somewhere a corporate decision system enabling us to do so. But there is no such thing. The Organization for Economic Co-operation and Development (OECD) is not a collective decision-making body: it is a consultative body. Even the Common Market is not a decision-making body, and neither, in my opinion, strictly speaking, is COMECON [4] or its successor. What we have are merely more or less integrated national projects.

Thus the prospects for the year 2000 are already latent in the weighty decisions being made at the present time with regard to these last twenty-five years of the century, and not at all in technological extrapolation. We must in fact look to the policies being formulated by the different governments in relation to each other and, occasionally, with each other, to discern the outlook for the year 2000; and from this point of view, I can only look ahead with pessimism.

I do not believe, I repeat, that China, the U.S.S.R., Japan, Western Europe, the United States and possibly the larger developing countries such as India and Brazil can reconcile their national policies on the type of society they propose to achieve.

There are and will be inconsistencies which will be reflected in shortages, critical thresholds, financial crises, etc. It is my belief that the best way to face the challenge of the year 2000 is to review our projections of consumption and bring our production and consumption potential back down to what, in terms of our ecological environment, can be deemed a normal level. For there is not *a* world consumption system, but *a variety* of world consumption systems. Our

fairly large number of new markets capable of providing the industrialized countries with manpower and trade outlets. To improve the lot of all peoples: this was the fundamental economic principle which would guarantee peace.... I wanted to have a clause inserted in the Young Plan making it compulsory for all the contracting parties to set up a bank whose task would be to distribute the sums paid by way of reparations and to carry out international financial operations with a view to providing the new countries with the resources essential for the development of their raw materials and the expansion of their agricultural production.... Co-operation between the vanquished and the victors within the framework of the Bank would give rise to a community of interests which would foster mutual understanding and help to maintain peace ... Dr Young's face lit up and his resolve was echoed in these words: "Dr Schacht, you have given me a wonderful idea and I am going to sell it to the world!" ' This scene took place in the late spring of 1929 and is quoted from Dr Schacht's memoirs, *76 Jahre Meines Lebens* (Munich, Kindler & Schiermeyer, 1950).

4 COMECON: Council for Mutual Economic Assistance of the socialist countries. Set up in Moscow in January 1949 to counterbalance the Marshall Plan. There are nine member countries: Bulgaria, Cuba, Czechoslovakia, the German Democratic Republic, Hungary, Mongolia, Poland, Romania, the U.S.S.R., and an associate member, Yugoslavia.

object should be to make, as it were, a critical analysis of the past twenty-five years.

In the last twenty-five years, as has been so eloquently pointed out, what has happened is that consumption has doubled in the developed countries. This is true of France, for example, where, as you are well aware, the real material standard of living in terms of housing, travel, energy, etc., has in fact doubled. And it is true of other Western nations. It has also been said that this rate of growth cannot continue. I share that view, but I will even go a step further and say that it was exceptional, indeed pure accident, that it should have doubled at all. I am convinced that it will never do so again, even on the present-day scale. And the greatest, most imperative challenge, to my mind, is the inevitable restriction of consumption. I am in entire agreement on that point. I cannot see how it can be increased.

What can be done constructively, however, is for the rich countries to examine the poorer nations' projects for society and help them achieve their goals in certain fundamental areas such as general facilities, education, and the meeting of some of their basic needs, to give us another twenty-five years, a generation, say, of breathing space, during which time technological advances may enable us to deal more comprehensively with the problems of humanity as a whole.

To sum up, I believe that the concerted global approach can only be regarded as a token, a sort of model or simulation, but that the underlying political realities are very different. I am not even alluding here to capitalist or socialist types of society, however much they may be, and indeed are, bound up with problems of shortage and surplus, as we well know. But what I do say is that powers of decision exist in the world today in the shape of nation-States, great or small, and that these nation-States carry on planning as though they could settle their differences by dint of sweeping general formulae and symposia of this kind. I, for one, claim that their present goals are incompatible, and that the time has come to analyse them.

New risks, new solutions

Trygve Bratteli

Personally, I do not believe too much in attempts to draw up specific and detailed drafts of the various parts of society in the year 2000. It will be a new generation who has to make the concrete decisions. But the general attitude towards such problems all around the world is marked by pessimism, and my first question is this: if we study human history over the last 100–150 years, is it not reasonable to suppose that the most important event is mankind's having produced weapons powerful enough to annihilate itself?

But I really want to know if this is the most important conclusion of such a study of the history of the last 100–150 years? At least quite a lot of other things have happened at the same time and if I am very loath to adopt this very pessimistic conclusion as to the future, it is because for me the most important thing that ever happened, and I think more markedly in the last 100 years, is the ability of man to be able to make decisions with respect to his own destiny; man's ability to face the problems of his time and, now I am convinced, those of the year 2000 and beyond. Most important is that man be able to meet the new period confident of this ability to solve his problems and the new problems that will arise in the coming decades. And if we examine the results, the consequences of scientific, economic, social development in the last generations, I personnally do not find ground for general pessimism as to the future. When I stress this, it is because I am looking for motivation for all the new generations to come, and I personally do not think that the prospect of a great catastrophe provides good motivation. Fear does not provide positive motivation in the forming of a new and better world, which for new generations should be a sensible programme and give life new meaning. I think it would be much better if motivation were based on historical grounds and on the certainty that coming generations will be able to solve the problems they encounter in the further development of modern society.

As has been said before, the coming generations will have to handle some very serious problems. Solutions to those problems will have to be found. But I think that with broader information as to the actual results of the long-term development of modern society, it will be much easier to organize the forces we need, and to cope convincingly with new problems as they arise.

I would like to stress this because I am afraid that if, in planning for the coming decades, we concentrate too much on the possibility of total catastrophe,[1] we will make further difficulties for ourselves which will be poor inspiration for assuming future responsibilities.

So even if this is not perhaps the way one should speak nowadays, I confess I am speaking as a politician for I am not a scientist or even semi-scientist. I am a politician who believes that if he is to survive and the people he is working for are to survive, the very positive elements in human development and the development of human society over the last generation must be found: this to my mind is the best reason for approaching coming problems with optimism.

I am not going into any detail as to the problem of the appropriate place for all people in the society in which they live, their proper place in industry, in employment and also their proper place in society generally. I have worked my whole life. I belong to the generation of Norwegians who spent three of the best years of its life in the ranks of the unemployed, at the beginning of the 1930s. I know what it is and very few things seem to me as alarming as the new tendency to widespread unemployment in many countries, even in the countries best prepared to handle such problems. Besides the fear of the great total catastrophe and some other problems which are sure to arise, I think the most important problem in our highly industrialized world in the coming twenty years will be providing proper employment and proper possibilities for the new generations which are now growing up.

1 In connection with this reservation by the Former Norwegian Prime Minister, and to offset various scenarios for the future, it may be noted that, for several years past, certain economists have been doing some soul-searching on the concepts of economics itself. They are particularly critical of the excessive use of mathematical models of a system, which, in their opinion, cause a block. They denounce certain theoretical shortcomings together with the mythology of figures and statistics. A movement of United States economists, the Union for Radical Political Economy, seeks to define a juster society by replacing the traditional objective of production-maximizing growth by that of redistribution of power and wealth, resulting in genuine equality of opportunity. The Union for Radical Political Economy was founded in 1967 and now has 2,500 members (Address: 41 Union Square West, Room 901, New York 10003 (United States).)

Discovering the art of living

Léon Boissier-Palun

The year 2000. Twenty-three years from now. A generation. It is also a continuation and fulfilment of today.

But we live in a world where things evolve very fast, a world in which revolution succeeds revolution, sometimes, almost without our noticing it.

It is also a world in which the threat of annihilation hangs over the human race. I remember when I was young, just before the last world catastrophe. I was a student in Bordeaux, and my mind was full of certainties. First among them was the certainty of living in a society where there was stability, including a monetary stability which enabled people to build the future and be sure of the fruits which their labour would certainly bring them. And when the clash of arms was heard to the east of France, just before the summer holidays which preceded that famous September of 1939, our professor called us together and said: 'As you know, this is perhaps the last time I shall see you. It's not a tragedy—all men's lives have to end some time. What worries me is that, when you come back, all the scales of value will have changed.'

At that time we believed in the virtue of power. We had been taught that glory was the goal of existence, that war did not mean suffering for other people, while for us it meant satisfaction and honour. To die was 'the finest and most enviable fate we had been told; and anyway, it was never we ourselves but always other people who actually died.

Life has taught me that our professor was absolutely right: since the war, many things have changed. The idea of good and evil has altered, social rules have been turned upside down, hierarchies called in question, the family more or less broked up. Our conviction that we lived in an unchanging society, with a strong currency which enabled us to build a future, has been swept away by uncertainty. The unrest of present-day youth is the product of uncertainty. Is not the challenge of the year 2000 therefore, likely to be ethical rather than material?

I have no wish to deny either that society is badly arranged and resources unequally distributed, or the necessity of overhauling economics and creating a new international economic order. I do not deny the nuclear threat, or the kind of self-destruction man is organizing around himself by destroying his environment. But in my view none of all that is really tragic: man is not lacking in intellectual resources, and the mind always finds a solution to any kind of difficulty.

What matters, it seems to me, is that the solutions found should be directed to securing man's happiness. The only reason for trying to build a world is that man may live happily in it himself and be happy in the happiness of others.

We have seen decolonization, the granting of independence, the proclamation of freedom for all, the proclamation of the dignity of man. And yet, every day, it all needs to be done over again because of the desire for domination on the part of a certain minority, whether of knowledge or of power.

The idea of happiness seems to me to have been distorted. For a long time man has sought happiness in the accumulation of wealth, regarding this as a guarantee of his future; while at the same time he has done nothing to check his own egoism, and in seeking his own security has jeopardized that of others. The same is true of the accumulation of weapons. In my opinion, therefore, the decisive revolution needs to take place in men's minds.

Since we are meeting in Unesco, it is fitting to refer to the Organization's Constitution, which says that 'since wars begin in the minds of men, it is in the minds of men that the defences of peace must be constructed'.

I believe that the happiness of a life, the happiness of life itself, consists not in the accumulation of wealth for wealth's sake, but in the liberation of man by new techniques which lighten his work and enlarge the possibilities of a life so short a time ago confined to labour; and also in the other liberation resulting from the creation of wealth which guarantees man's survival. But most of us have to live in developed societies which offer no other goal but the race for possessions. People forget more and more that the important thing is to live.

It is true that the laying down of a number of principles or the proclaiming of a set of rules will effect no overnight improvement. Even that still remains to be done. In my view there is only one way, and that is through the knowledge which enables every man to choose. All sorts of equalities have been proclaimed, including equality of access to education and knowledge, but science and technology have developed so far since the Second World War that now, when Paris sneezes, Peking catches cold,[1] and the means of communication have developed in such a way that, unless they are freed from interference by powerful interests, they will become means of enslavement.

Between 1950 and 1960 there was what was called the Development Decade, which stressed economic development and the need for a more equitable distribution of the world's goods. I think we now need to stress the right of every individual and every group to participate freely in the means of communication.

The driving force in the mental revolution will probably come from a revolution in the media of communication.

When everyone is fully informed and is able to inform others, then perhaps we shall see the birth of sensibility, creativity and art, and perhaps also of the happiness of life, which will give us time to think, and above all, time to waste.

It may be that Africa, if it can direct its own information towards Europe, will be able to teach this part of the world something about the art of living and of wasting time.

[1] 'Ours is a brand-new world of instantaneity. "Time" has ceased "space" has vanished. We live now in a global village ... a simultaneous happening....

'Unhappily, we confront this new situation with an enormous backlog of outdated mental and psychological responses.... Our most impressive words and thoughts betray us—they refer us only to the past, not to the present.

'Electric circuitry profoundly involves men with one another. Information pours upon us, instantaneously and continuously.... Our electrically configured world has forced us to move from the habit of data classification to the mode of pattern recognition. We can no longer build serially, block-by-block, step-by-step, because instant communication ensures that all factors of the environment and of experience co-exist in a state of active interplay.'— H. Marshall McLuhan, *The Medium is the Message*, p. 63, London, Allen Lane and Penguin Press, 1967.

Unforeseen challenges

Tewfik Al-Hakim

The challenges of the year 2000 are so enormous and so complicated that I scarcely feel competent to confront them. So I shall confine myself to a rapid consideration of one of the most urgent problems, one which is at present causing concern to everyone: the problem of energy. Its seriousness lies in the fact that, if we do not succeed in solving it, it will jeopardize human progress.

We are apparently all more or less agreed that the most immediate solution is the discovery of new energy resources to avoid being dependent on a single source which may dry up, like oil. Solar and nuclear energy and other types produced by modern technology are already in use. And here I come to the greatest challenge of the year 2000—the word 'technology'. Technology carried to an extreme may threaten to destroy another source of energy nowadays neglected: the energy produced by men's muscles. Modern man more and more allows himself to be replaced even for his most trivial needs, by mechanical power. Even in underdeveloped or developing countries, electricity consumption will have doubled or tripled by the end of the century. In other words, man everywhere, in the deserts, the countryside and the towns, is gradually making less and less use of his natural strength. If man's indolence makes him neglect human energy and rely entirely on mechanical energy to the point where he is finally replaced by machines, we shall begin the next century with the proclamation that 'Man is dead', just as Nietzsche said in the nineteenth century that God [1] was dead.

To save man from this terrible fate, we must begin now to find a way of establishing a wise and careful balance between

1 'The Newtonian God—the God who made a clocklike universe, wound it, and withdrew—died a long time ago. This is what Nietzsche meant and this is the God who is being observed.

'Anyone who is looking around for a simulated icon of the deity in Newtonian guise might well be disappointed. The phrase "God is dead" applies aptly, correctly, validly to the Newtonian universe which is dead. The ground rule of that universe, upon which so much of our Western world is built, has dissolved.'—Marshall McLuhan, *The Medium is the Message*.

human and mechanical energy. We must educate or re-educate the people of the next century not to rely on machines except where their own strength is inadequate. The object here is apt not only to economize artificial energy but also to preserve the physical abilities and moral virtues of the human race, and defend natural man against the invasion of mechanical man.

For energy is the symbolic image of civilization, and it is terrible to think that the civilization of a future century will be the civilization of mechanical man. Just as Nietzsche's nineteenth-century verdict on God is now answered by contemporary thinkers who proclaim that 'God exists', so let us hope that the warning cry about man will be answered by the declaration that 'Man is alive'.

Religion is another of the problems likely to arise in the year 2000. What will be the relationship between religion and science? Religion, which is peculiar to man alone, answers the eternal question he has asked himself throughout the ages: 'Who created the world?' Could the atheistic science of the previous century become, in the next, a science which has faith? I realize that the word 'religion' and even the word 'God' as conceived by scientists could not have the same meaning or foundation as are attributed to them by the clergy. But the question still has to be asked, for it is the perpetual question of mankind. Every century asks it, and the next century will ask it when the time comes, even on other planets and in other galaxies. Who created the universe? If science is silent, religion speaks. If science were to speak in the affirmative, I cannot foresee what place religion would take. It might perhaps be possible to combine the scientist and the priest in one man, like the priest of Amon in the days of the Pharaohs.

At all events, should we or should we not put the relationship between science and religion on the list of problems for the year 2000? I should like to hear the opinion of that eminent scientist Professor Alfred Kastler. [2]

Another question concerns the word 'progress'. Does it need to be given a new meaning? Is the march of mankind like the course of the earth round the sun—not linear but circular? Is there always an eternal return? For example, is not the architecture of the pharaoh's pyramids based on a geometric figure forming a massive triangular block, repeated in modern architecture, for example, in the geometrical aesthetics of the great rectangular block of the Tour Montparnasse in Paris? I leave the question to those competent to judge. What I wish to stress is primarily the need to revise the meaning, conception and application of the word 'progress'.

2 Written reply from Professor Kastler:
'Mr Tewfik Al-Hakim asked my opinion about the relationship between science and religion. I do not think there is any contradiction between these two spiritual activities of man. They are complementary. Science and religion exist at different levels of spiritual activity. Science belongs to the realm of knowledge, of the study of facts accessible to our senses. Religion belongs to the realm of faith. In every age there have been scientists who were believers, and scientists who were not.
'I should like to question one of the expressions used by Mr Al-Hakim. He speaks of the "atheistic science of the previous century". I do not think this is correct. The nineteenth century saw the development of a philosophical trend known as "scientific materialism". Some people, basing their argument on the still very incomplete findings of science, thought they could deduce that God did not exist. This is an illusion. The existence of God, of a creator of the world, can be neither demonstrated nor disproved by science. Science is neither religious nor anti-religious. It is a-religious. It seeks to explain the evolution of the world by the "principle of causality". The believer asserts that there is a "principle of finality" present in the universe. These two principles are complementary and not contradictory, and both were conceived by the human mind.'

What we have to ask ourselves first is: progress in relation to what or to whom? Animals know how to adapt means to ends. They use only the necessary amount of muscular energy, wasting none. In the same way, they economize food. There is no squandering. A lion buries the remain of his prey to provide future meals, though he nobly leaves part of it to animals poorer, i.e. weaker, than himself. Animals are also wise enough not to provoke aggressive wars in order to dominate and to impose their way of living and thinking on others. But men still do not know how to adapt their means to their ends. They heedlessly squander their natural and mechanical energies, and compensate for their lack of equilibrium by technological and ideological means which, when they are successful, they call progress.

Like many other words and definitions which seem stable and lasting, then, the word 'progress' needs to be revised. So does what is called a country's 'national independence'. This generally means that each country shuts itself up within its own interests, leaving out of account the interests which all people have in common all over the world. Is it so difficult to imagine the possibility, one day, of gathering together the governments of every country in the world so that they might together, impartially, watch over the interests and the future of mankind in general? If, despite differences of nationality, religion and race, Unesco can gather us together here to consider the problems of humanity as a whole, why should we not hope for a similar gathering at the level of leaders from all over the globe? A redefinition of 'national independence' might bring the realization of that hope nearer.

To conclude, I fear that, if we do not revise all the assumptions of our present-day civilization, we are in for some unexpected challenges from the year 2000.

Man—humanity's only hope

Peter Ustinov

To those of us too nervous or too ill-informed to think with global clarity of the year 2000, it is wise to think of tomorrow, of even late this afternoon which is really the same thing, but somehow more accessible. It goes without saying that creatures who are inhibited by the very idea of the year 2000 will also be unable to assimilate the staggering figures of population explosion and gross national product or lack of it, or debt, any more than they could assimilate the monumental casualties of the last war. Wholesale figures are matters for experts trained to deal with them on easy and relaxed terms. The rest of us tend to shudder momentarily, but it takes an individual case of injustice, of intolerance, or of achievement to reduce the facts to the dimensions compatible with our emotions. Why is this? Is it not perhaps because there is a realization in even the most politically rigid of us that whereas the toiling masses are a fine concept for the words of the average national anthem or for the speech of a workaday demagogue, the individual is intrinsically more important than any crowd of people. The individual is the currency of our comprehension Everything is correctly judged by the needs, the morality, the opportunities, the rights of the individual.

The Rights of Man—not the Rights of Men. The masses are an amorphous collection of individuals who have momentarily lost their voice in the general chaos, and as such resemble in their way, the huge statistics which challenge our comprehension. There is not an idea, good or bad, which was not born in the mind of a single man or woman, in fact, brain children is an apt if rather affected description of ideas, they grow from embryos in the minds of individuals. A collectivity, a council, a committee, a junta, *force majeure* can alter, improve, destroy or immortalize an idea, but they cannot have it. And, to mollify those who may bridle at the insolence of my ideas, remember that the idea of the resurgence of the working class did not come from the working class itself, but from the mind of a single man, Karl Marx. The masses may well have awakened from their slumbers, but it was Karl Marx who wound the alarm clock, perhaps Plekhanov who indicated where it should be placed, and Lenin who set the time.

Perhaps this will serve to explain why I have taken an opposite course to the brilliant and tumultuous one of Buckminster Fuller, who speaks to the elements much as Orpheus sang to the wild beasts, or of those magnificent orators who launch their ideas into the stratosphere of acute perception from launching pads of superior competence. All these are experts, and feel at home with the vaster generalities, with graphs, and the elucidation of mathematics.

While paying them unswerving attention, I feel the need to swing to the other extreme, and to speculate briefly on how that vulnerable creature man will fare in the age of efficiency which has begun to envelop him.

First of all, it must be clear to any but the most unrelenting statistician that the year 2000 is an arbitrary landmark, for even today there are nations mentally and physically in the twelfth century as there are those greedily reaching for the twenty-first. There are leaders who are in search of tangible immortality, or at least of Shakespeare. And yet, who are we to scoff? Have we not passed through the Dark Ages in the exhausting processes of maturity, today accelerated unnaturally by the terrifying speed of technical advance in an indivisible world? The year 2000 is a reality for a handful of nations. For others, it is the twelfth, thirteenth, fourteenth, fifteenth century, and perhaps most dangerous of all, the nineteenth and the early twentieth century. Before we smile at the eccentric accelerations of natural processes, the military traditions invented overnight, the anthems with bombastic words and catchpenny tunes, the fantastic uniforms, let us admit how fragile we ourselves are, and how beneath the business suit, lingers the body of a human animal, whereas the cranium of *homo sapiens* is but an improvement on the prototype of Neanderthal and a symphonic variation on a speck of caviar in a muddy pond.

We pride ourselves that the era of colonialism in its physical sense is over even if colonialism has emerged in

other forms. This may be true of land—and yet look at the
sordid drama of the sea. A look at the sordid drama of the
sea should chasten us before we breathe a sigh of relief. The
sea used to be a place devoid of frontiers. A drowning man
was rescued as a matter of principle before it was possible to
ask him his religion or his beliefs. It was even possible—
and for a little time still will be—for a warship to visit a
foreign port on a goodwill visit. Who ever heard of a
goodwill division marching into a foreign town?

Now, since the end of *terra incognita*, it is the time of
mare incognitum. From three to twelve to fifty miles out to
sea stretch the tentacles of man's natural and possessive
instincts, and soon the available space will be taken by
squatters in the form of nuclear submarines, oil rigs, and
other toys of a prolonged adolescence, wallowing in their
own pollution.

And if it were only nations—but no, they too are often
in peril themselves. Diplomacy is by now merely a matter
of charming protocol—its place in the age of efficiency has
been usurped by the business deal, the mysteries of multinational corporations which started humbly with rubber and
bananas in certain proscribed places on the map, but which
since have extended their activities to the disruption of much
larger national entities, lending their incalculable weight to
political tendencies with the tacit approval of some governments and the calculated silence of others. Such companies,
run with admirable efficiency, often became multinational in
order to escape from the rigours of antitrust laws, and are
able to function internationally in a manner which would
never be tolerated at home.

Is it not self-evident that with such inducements, with
such undercurrents and with the replacement of diplomacy
by what are known as business ethics, numerous international
financial scandals and even Watergate [1] are the logical consequences of this tendency? Who is to blame for this? No one,
of course. They are the logical consequences of evolution
—and of a noble experiment in personal human freedom which
lifted the restraints from man, and encouraged him to run
before he could walk, if that is what came naturally to him.

Naturally also, together with the immense surge of
inventions which benefit mankind, great advances in medicine
and in discovery and in general convenience—things which
were difficult if not impossible for the political theorists of
the last century to envisage—there have come the contingent
advances in weaponry, in articles of wholesale destruction,
of limited and terminal utility. But, since we deal not only
with nations but also with businessmen, not only with

1 On 17 June 1972 five
burglars were arrested while
rifling the files in the offices
of the Democratic Party
headquarters in the Watergate Hotel in Washington,
D.C. When it was discovered
that the five were employed
by members of the White
House staff of President
Nixon—the operation had
been planned and carried
out with funds channeled for
the purpose from the Nixon
re-election campaign com-
mittee—the episode became
known internationally as the
Watergate Scandal, and
ultimately forced the resignation of President Nixon.
Nixon resigned to avoid
impeachment on the charge
of obstructing justice. The
evidence supporting the
charge was contained in the
White House tapes of the
president's and others'
conversations relevant to the
issue. Nixon refused to
deliver the tapes to the
Senate Investigating Com-
mittee until the Supreme
Court found unanimously
against him on the issue.
The involvement of both
the CIA and the FBI in the
attempt to cover up the
scandal resulted in the
investigation, reform and
widespread curtailment of
both these organizations
while Nixon's resignation
led directly to the installation
of his appointed vice-
president, Gerald Ford, in
the presidency.

manufacturers but with retailers, and eventually with street hawkers, there is not only the secret, restricted market of the overkill—but more reprehensible still, and perhaps finally more dangerous, the market in obsolescent weapons, in advanced trainer aircraft disguised as fighters, in vulnerable tanks, in spare parts, for sale to the developing countries for the sake of appearances and for the conduct of local wars over which the great powers cast a nostalgic and avuncular eye, and eventually express concern.

And since this is the Age of Efficiency, the spectrum is further clouded by a pragmatic collusion between the super-powers despite the usual appearance of friction and hostility and, once again, it is natural that countries linked by their enormous power and size should have problems in common that smaller powers do not have, and further that world opinion, witnessing spellbound the drama on the stage without being privy to the whispered conversations in the wings, should develop double standards. The same collusion exists on every level of power. The European powers cluster together and attempt to speak in unison in order to give more resonance to their voice, while the non-aligned nations recognize the dangers of a world divided into two major camps, and try to provide a little ventilation into the over-charged atmosphere. Then there are the regional and racial blocs founded, much as trade unions were founded, for collective protection in the chilling world of commercial colonialism, that new form of external preponderance which seems so different to its perpetrators and so similar to its recipients, investments with invisible strings attached instead of soldiers with visible bayonets fixed. Power has become abstract rather than absent. It is present in our creature comforts and in our food.

But of course, the failures, the shortcomings during an age of efficiency must, by definition, take the form of inefficiency. Buckminster Fuller, an authority worthy of the closest attention by virtue of his undeniable and colossal achievements, has already stated that 99 per cent of humanity have no idea what technology is all about. Being cautious by nature and by virtue of my total ignorance of the subject in hand, I would be willing to accept the figure of 98 per cent. This is still a figure somewhat on the large side. But I must say, once again, as a layman, that I am consistently amazed by the divergence of opinions among distinguished economists, whose arguments I attempt to follow at a respectful distance. We only have to read the papers to observe economists indulging in verbal conflict all the time. One of them only has to express an opinion for a whole pack of

them to descend on him with the flattest, the most urgent
contradictions. One would have thought, would one not,
that at this stage of evolution, economics would have become
a more exact science rather than a field as rich in cries of
heresy as when the first shy voices suggested the earth was
not flat after all.

Is this not perhaps nature's teasing retaliation to our
raping of her secrets. The more we know, the more we
discover how much there still is left to know. The family
doctor used to be an irrefutable oracle. His medicine was
prescribed, and if you died, it was clearly your fault.

Nowadays, the doctor is a man like you, only more
anxious, because he is not ill. He gives you pills, and he says:
'If your nose begins to bleed, or partial paralysis sets in,
stop taking them at once, call me at any hour of the day or
night and we'll try something else'. Then he gives you five
possible telephone numbers at which he can be reached,
and rushes to his next appointment. If you should be
forced to ring, you will find him between two numbers, but
which two the nurse or the answering service is unable to
tell you.

There we have it. The Age of Efficiency is fraught with
stress and nervousness, while ever advancing are the waves
of youth disappointed with the world we have brought them
into, not as yet hardened to its social habits, struggling for
diplomas which are no longer guarantees of jobs, incredulous
of our hypocritical assurances that all they need to do is to
follow in our footsteps, footsteps which have been washed
away by time and tide.

The young are remarkably similar in outlook and in
spirit all the world over. They are the only really spontaneous
proof of the possibilities of human co-operation, made all
the more tantalizing for being ephemeral. Once they join us
in the morass of commitment and cacaphony, they are as
lost as we are, but mercifully replaced by a new wave as a
permanent symbol of elusive hope.

I am not qualified to predict with any greater lucidity or
prescience what awaits man in the year 2000. I have access
to no figures. I am in the cosy company of the 98 per cent
who do not understand technology. I only know that,
now that telephones link all parts of the globe, more
and more people telephone me for absolutely no reason,
the monotony of this sometimes graciously mitigated by the
recorded voice of a pleasant lady saying: '*Les lignes sont
surchargées. Veuillez essayer plus tard.*'

I am not so much concerned with what man will achieve,
as I am concerned by what man risks to lose—his life, among

other things, in some careless holocaust; his voice, in the crowd; his dignity, as a slave to his standards of living.

You live and learn, I hope, more at my age than when I was young. You realize that all news is, by its very nature, tendentious. It is better to read two newspapers than one. There can be little argument here, since this is good for business. It is even better to read three newspapers than two, preferably in different languages.

You find out daily things you did not know, even outside Unesco. You find out, for instance, that the inquiry into the death of the only soldier to be shot for cowardice in the Western theatre of operations in the last war, is to be reopened.[2] In the course of this investigation, it is revealed that he lies buried in the corner of a cemetery reserved for the dishonoured. You do not have to be versed in the delicacy of military law to ask yourself if this eternal damnation is not a violation of human rights as grave and as squalid as those practised on the living in every corner of the globe. A mere incident perhaps, and a sentimental one at that, and yet no incident in this existence is worthy of neglect any more than the millions of individuals which constitute the human race are. The 40,000 deep-frozen Korean embryos subjected to military experiments are but a modern expression of the mentality which relegates a corpse to eternal disgrace—not so much immoral as, what is worse, amoral.

You find out that your faith in man as a thinking creature evolving rather slower than his environment, but with his freedom of thought inviolate in the depths of his being, is undiminished, even if your faith in men, bustled into national, regional, political, and now corporate loyalties is under permanent strain, Still, it is man who is important, his capacity for thinking for himself, and of assuming responsibility.

2 In January 1945, Eddy E. Slovik, an American soldier, was shot at Sainte-Marie-aux-Mines (France) on a charge of repeated desertion. The affair made news again recently when his widow claimed a service pension (see the *International Herald Tribune* of 1 July 1977 and *The Execution of the Private Eddy E. Slovik*, by William Bradford Huie, 1954).

Man against
the powers that be

The super-nuclear arms monster

Philip Noel-Baker

Christopher Fry, an English poet, wrote in a poem entitled *A Sleep of Prisoners*: 'Behind us lies the thousand and the thousand and the thousand years, vexed and terrible. And still we use the cures that never cure.' [1]

Today, we know the cures that cure. We have seen them work. The challenge of 2000, many have said it, is 'shall we get there?' 'Or shall we perish on the way?' Shall we get there?

I feel sick with apprehension when I think of the dangers that lie ahead for the year 2000. But I feel still more sick with remorse when I remember the opportunities of the past that we have lost. It is the nuclear arms race that may destroy us. But not nuclear only. It is the guns as well as the nuclear bombs that may destroy us. Hitler fought a war that lasted six years, that brought the world to utter chaos. There were no nuclear weapons in his armoury, it was with what we call conventional bombers, conventional artillery, conventional machine-guns, that he destroyed the world. But the nuclear arms race is the crux today. And let me try to tell you to what point of frenzy it has reached. I have a friend, Dr Herbert York, who was for years the chief scientist in the Pentagon. He wrote in 1973 that the nuclear stockpile of the United States was 15,000 megatons. Do you understand the meaning? In six years of war the allied forces dropped 1.2 million tons on Germany, and Germany from north to south, from east to west, was a ruin. And one megaton is a million tons of TNT—1.2 million in six years of aerial bombing. One million in a second of time and from a single bomber.

1 *A Sleep of Prisoners*, a work by Christopher Fry, the poet and playwright, was published in 1940.

Dr Frank Barnaby, the head of the Stockholm International Peace Research Institute (SIPRI) [2] in Stockholm, has calculated that 400 weapons of one megaton each, used on the Soviet Union, would kill 80 million people and destroy two-thirds of Soviet industry. Four hundred megatons, 3 per cent of the United States stockpile, 97 per cent unused, and 80 million dead. But he says that if you went on using megatons, you will get what the economist calls a diminishing return. Fewer dead per megaton than you got at first. But when you reach 6,000 then every Russian and every animal and every creeping thing in Russia, has died. It is a radioactive desert. Six thousand megatons, 40 per cent of Herbert York's present United States stockpile of nuclear bombs, 60 per cent unused, 60 per cent, 9,000 megatons that can do no Russian any harm.

You cannot kill a Russian twice. But nuclear weapons are not like artillery shells. You fire a sixteen-inch shell —I was there often at the point where they arrived in the First World War—you fire a sixteen-inch shell, you will destroy a mighty building, you kill a hundred people, but that is the end. Not so with nuclear weapons. You destroy the object, you murder Hiroshima with a nuclear midget. In a morning, 240,000 people die. A quarter of a million. And many die, they are dying still from the effects of that first nuclear bomb. But it is not the end. The mushroom cloud of a megaton bomb rises 40,000 feet towards the heavens, they are mushroom clouds across the wall of heaven—are the writing which says: 'By this the race of man may die.' For the upper winds take the deadly fall-out, they carry it back to the United Kingdom, France, across the broad Atlantic to the United States. And 60 per cent of the United States stockpile, the 9,000 megatons, if they were ever used, would be a deadly menace to Americans themselves. Americans have made the weapons, they have spent vast treasure in perfecting them. But if they use them, Americans will die. And if they use them all, the world will die.

What is the answer? President Jimmy Carter's is: zero nuclear weapons. But not zero nuclear weapons alone. General disarmament to prevent another Hitler's war. The demilitarization of the governments of the world. Yes, but how?

An ardent young Australian said to me in despair: 'How can we manage to get the disarmament we know to be desired? Everybody at home tells me, oh, that's Utopian, the climate of opinion must be changed, the climate of confidence must be created, all that is Utopian.' Face to

2 SIPRI, the Stockholm International Peace Research Institute, is an independent research institute concerned with the problem of war and peace. It concentrates particularly on disarmament and arms limitation. SIPRI was founded in 1966 to mark a century and a half of uninterrupted peace in Sweden. It is financed by the Swedish Parliament. The team of research workers, the Board and the Scientific Council are recruited internationally. As an advisory body, the Scientific Council is not responsible for the views expressed in the publications of SIPRI, whose present Director, Frank Barnaby, is British.

3 Woodrow Wilson (1856–1924), American politician, was President of the United States from 1912 to 1921. He was the author of the famous 'fourteen points' (including the reduction of armaments and the establishment of the League of Nations).

4 Lord Robert Cecil (1864–1958) was one of the main drafters of the League of Nations covenant and a staunch advocate of collective security and the limitation of armaments.

5 General Smuts (1870-1950), South African politician. At the 1919 Peace Conference he became the 'mandate man' in reference to the system established at this instance for the colonies of the conquered countries by the 1919 peace treaties and the League of Nations covenant. There were three categories of mandates: (a) those applying to areas detached from the Ottoman Empire (Syria, Lebanon, Palestine, Mesopotamia), in fact an assistance mandate; (b) those applying to peoples dependent on the Mandatory State (Togo, Cameroon, German East Africa); (c) States or territories placed under the legislation of the mandatory power. The United Nations replaced mandates by the trusteeship system (1946).

6 Eric Drummond (1876–1951). First Secretary-General of the League of Nations.

7 Fridthof Nansen (1861–1930). Norwegian explorer. League of Nations High Commissioner for the repatriation of prisoners of war (1921–23), for Russian refugees, and for refugees (1924). The Nansen organization introduced the Nansen passport, which in theory gave the holder the

face with his despair, I remember the words of Winston Churchill: 'If you say the past is the past, you have surrendered the future.' So I talk about the past. I was a Secretary of the Peace Commission here in Paris, which in 1919 wrote the covenant of the League of Nations. I sat with Woodrow Wilson. [3] I listened to Robert Cecil [4] and General Smuts. [5] I saw the covenant come alive. I joined the secretariat of the League of Nations. I went with Eric Drummond [6] to Geneva. I worked with Robert Cecil and with Fridtjof Nansen. [7] I saw the League become what Edward Benes called it: the greatest concept ever conceived within the human mind. I saw the League of Nations come to full success.

I saw what confidence the people had in it in 1934 and 1935 when we had a peace ballot in the United Kingdom. Eleven million people answered six questions in writing. Ninety-seven per cent were in favour of the country remaining in the League; 93 per cent were for a treaty of general world disarmament; 85 per cent were for the abolition of the air forces provided all nations did it too; 93 per cent were for economic sanctions against aggression; 74 per cent—three out of four—were for military sanctions if they should be required to stop aggression. I was at Geneva, as assistant to the president of the conference in 1932, when the spokesmen of the world gathered to carry through the disarmament ordained by Article 8 of the covenant we had drafted in Paris in the Hotel de Crillon. I saw the spokesmen of 1,000 million people—churches, trade unions, co-operative members, women's organizations, students—the spokesmen of 1,000 million people, demand that the conference should succeed.

And a little later, I saw the veterans of the First World War, two organizations—CIAMAC [8] and FIDAC [9]—which never joined together, never took a common action, except to send the delegation to the disarmament conference that would save the world. A delegation—5,000 men. And when they marched through the streets of old Geneva, the first fifty files were soldiers in wheelchairs. They had lost their legs, they had lost their arms, they were blinded, they had their heads smashed by enemy shells. I heard their spokesmen demand during the conference that it should not dissolve until it had carried through the abolition of the armaments with which the First World War had ruined their lives.

The League of Nations succeeded, it made the Permanent Court of International Justice. The court gave forty decisions, every one faithfully carried out by the disputing

States. It settled innumerable disputes that did not go to law. And then I saw the League break up, I saw the betrayal of Manchuria, [10] when militarists of Japan, who killed the Prime Minister of Japan, the grandfather of our friend Michiko Inukai, because he opposed what they were doing in their aggression against China. I saw the League betrayed. I saw the disarmament conference fail. I saw the League betrayed again when Mussolini made a second aggression against the Emperor of the Ethiopians. [11] Who made those betrayals? How did they happen? I say it with shame, but I was a member of the British Foreign Office at the time—I was a Member of Parliament—it was the militarists, the hawks, the bureaucrats of the British Empire who destroyed the League. The British Empire—650 million people under the domination of the monarch in Buckingham Palace in London—was the most powerful military State in every continent in the world. Without the British Empire, the collective security of the League of Nations could not work. But with it, it was irresistible.

France, Germany, Italy, Scandinavia, the Netherlands, Belgium, the British Commonwealth—all would have been united in the mighty alliance against armaments and war, if Robert Cecil, if Arthur Balfour, [12] if General Smuts, if Arthur Henderson, [13] had had their way. But there was a small minority of hawks, a small minority of militarists and bureaucrats. I name them: Sir Maurice Hankey, Secretary of our Cabinet for twenty years, Secretary of our Committee of Imperial Defence, enormous influence with Prime Ministers, the Ministers of Defence; Sir Robert Vansittart, the Permanent Under-Secretary of State in our Foreign Office. I worked with them. I argued with them about their memorandums, I told them they were wrong about Manchuria, I told them they were wrong about the disarmament conference of 1932. I told them they were wrong in the crucial case of Abyssinia. But they worked against the League. Why?

They were honourable, patriotic men, but they believed in armaments and war. I have been reading what they wrote in our secret documents now open for historians to peruse. I have read the letters and the memoranda which Maurice Hankey sent to Robert Cecil, and he says: 'The military spirit is what matters most in the civilization we have achieved. Let the military spirit die, degeneracy sets in. Let the military spirit die and your civilization will be lost.' And the basic proposition of them all, however much the League of Nations may postpone it: war will come. It was that idea, that simple fact in the minds of the bureaucrats and the

right to remain in the country issuing the passport. In fact, that principle was challenged by various countries (including Greece).

8 CIAMAC: International Conference of Associations of War Cripples and Ex-Servicemen.

9 FIDAC: Inter-Allied Federation of Ex-Servicemen.

10 In the autumn of 1931, following sabotage on a railway, the imperial Japanese army invaded Manchuria, ostensibly to protect Japanese property and interests in the region (in fact there had been many more or less serious 'incidents' since 1928 and military operations had long been given mature consideration by the Japanese general staff). China appealed to the League of Nations, which invited Japan to evacuate the areas occupied by its troops in Manchuria. Japan took no notice and extended its areas of occupation. When the Chinese boycotted Japanese goods, Tokyo sent troops to Shanghai in January 1932. After several weeks of fighting, the Chinese withdrew from the Shanghai area. In the spring of 1932, the Japanese made Manchuria into a new state, Manchoukuo. In Tokyo, politicians opposed to the Japanese militarist machinations in Manchuria were shot down by the Ketsumeidon, a terrorist organization, and the Prime Minister himself, Inukai, perished on 15 March 1932. Manchuria was conquered by the U.S.S.R. in 1945 and reverted to China after the defeat of Japan.

militarists of the British Empire: war will come, it is inevitable. It was that idea that led them to destroy the League of Nations, to betray the British pledges, to make the catastrophic disaster of the Second World War. And when the Second World War was nearly won, Winston Churchill wrote a letter to Robert Cecil, in which he said: 'This war should be called the unnecessary war, it could easily have been prevented if the League of Nations had been upheld with courage and resolution by the associated nations.' And he meant the United Kingdom and France.

What lesson do I draw from that long history? A great French philosopher, Pascal, wrote: 'Opinion is the sovereign of the world.' [14] It's not the trends of history that historians talk about, it is not forces of nature, it is not accidents of good fortune or of evil fortune that determine the events that actually occur. It is what men think, it is what men believe, what happens in their minds. Let me try to make that idea really come alive.

What did it mean when Pascal wrote: Opinion is the sovereign of the world? It meant an absolute monarch whose slightest whim was law, who spent vast fortunes on building palaces, on keeping a costly court and costly mistresses; who ground the faces of the poor with monstrous taxes, who sent young men to death with mutilation in his senseless, ceaseless wars. It meant the Church, remarkable for spiritual indifference and moral sloth. It meant universities where learning languished, where dogma and fantasy took their place. It meant a caste of nobles who lived in idle luxury, making their peasants work for no wage at all, many, many days a year, taking the greater part of the crops the peasants produced. That was the way while Pascal was alive. It lasted until he died, it lasted for a century after he was gone. Why? Because the monarch, because the courtiers, because the Churches and the universities and the nobles, because the peasants themselves, all believed that it was God's ordering of the world. All believed it was how things had to be. And then, when a century had passed, Jean-Jacques Rousseau wrote, in *The Social Contract*: 'Men are born free and are everywhere in chains.' [15] He asked the question: Why?—Why are the peasants in serfdom to the nobles? Voltaire joined him with the sharp sword of satire. And in 1789 the monarch summoned the Three Estates to meet him at Versailles, and when he sent them home they refused to go. And on 14 July the Bastille was stormed, and then the nobles went to courts of people's justice established by the lower classes. The nobles went to people's courts of justice, they went in tumbrels to the

11 On 2 October 1935, the Negus announced by cable to the League of Nations that Ethiopia was under attack from Italian troops. The war lasted until May 1936. After the fall of Addis Ababa, Mussolini proclaimed Ethiopia Italian. The country was liberated in 1941 by the British army.

12 Lord Arthur Balfour (1848–1930) was Chairman of the Council of the League of Nations and attended the Washington Conference in 1921, where he proposed that submarines be abolished and that the debt of Germany and the allies to the United Kingdom be limited to the amount of the United Kingdom's debt to the United States. France refused.

13 Arthur Henderson (1863–1935) was President of the 1933 Geneva Disarmament Conference, when Philip Noel-Baker was his assistant.

14 '... Opinion is the sovereign of the world, but force is its tyrant'.—*Pensées*, Ch. V, Para. 5. In the same work (Ch. XXIV, Para. 91) Pascal writes: 'Force is the sovereign of the world and not opinion, but opinion is the user of force.'

15 *The Social Contract*, Book I, Chapter I, 1762.

16 The funeral oration for heroes who had died for their country was a purely civil act. The orator, appointed by the Senate, delivered it, reports Thucydides, after they had been buried in the Ceramicus, a district of guillotine and Frenchmen were never serfs again. And there came from that French Revolution the noblest of all human programmes of political action: liberty, equality, fraternity, which you see written on all the public buildings in Paris today.

And we have to ask the question: why are we in serfdom to militarist ideas of the past? We need a new, simple, strong idea. War is out of date. War is no longer practical politics. Militarism is a philosophy of the dead. Armaments are the toys of monarchs and of general staffs, they are the instruments of murder. They are out of date.

Can Unesco, can the United Nations, can we, help to make that simple, strong idea penetrate the consciousness of governments and peoples throughout the world? I believe we can. Three weeks ago today, Queen Elizabeth made a speech in the Guild Hall which should rank with the Periclean oration of Ancient Greece, [16] with the Gettysburg oration [17] that Lincoln pronounced in 1863. She spoke of the transformation of that mighty British Empire, the mightiest that history has ever known, of its transformation from an Empire into a Commonwealth of free and equal partners:

Events of history brought our nations of all races of all the continents together; but we have come to understand that instead of domination from the centre, we share a common humanity. We have learnt the courage to prefer compromise to conflict. We have learnt that our interests are common interests which, by common action, the Commonwealth can promote.

Can mankind now free itself from the serfdom of the militarist doctrines of the past? The Commonwealth has been transformed since the Queen became Queen, twenty-five years ago. We have twenty-five years before us, and if we can make that simple, strong idea prevail—that war is out of date—we shall make for all men a life far nobler and far fuller than any man has known before.

Athens. In 430 B.C. one year after the outbreak of the Peloponnesian war between Athens and Sparta, Pericles delivered a funeral oration which has gone down in history. He spoke to the Athenians not so much of heroes as of Athens: 'Numerous States have been formed on the model of ours; we ourselves copy nobody. The name of democracy is sufficient testimony to the purpose of our institutions, which is to serve the general interest and not that of a particular order of citizens.... The law is equal unto all.... In public affairs the spirit of liberty inspires our every act. Our city is open to all peoples; not for us such laws as debar the stranger... our courage is our sole refuge and we pour equal scorn on mystery and guile.... We are alone too, in wishing affairs to be judged and duly considered, in our conviction that discussion can bring no harm and that, in most undertakings, failure is due but to lack of prior enlightenment.'

17 On 19 November 1863, at Gettysburg (Pennsylvania) where the Northerners had won a victory over the Southern troops commanded by General Lee, Abraham Lincoln delivered the funeral oration now so famous: '... our fathers brought forth on this continent a new nation conceived in liberty and dedicated to the proposition that all men are created equal. Now we are engaged in a great civil war ... that these dead shall not have died in vain, that this nation ... shall have a new birth of freedom, and that government of the people, by the people, for the people, shall not perish from the earth.'

Solidarity still has to be achieved

André Fontaine

As I listened to President Echeverría, I recognized many themes that I myself have advocated, and that he advocated just as authoritatively when he was President of Mexico, particularly from the rostrum of the United Nations. It was thanks to him, I recall, that the document on the Charter of Economic Rights and Duties of States [1] was adopted, which sums up in the most precise detail what form the new world economic order may take: the Challenges of the year 2000! Do they not indeed boil down to one and the same challenge? What mankind has to do at the close of this century and the beginning of the next is to find out whether it can survive all the threats that confront it. For a catastrophe could occur even before the year 2000. This is the first time, in fact—and it can never be repeated too often—that mankind has had the means to destroy itself completely. It even has several times the means, since by a paradox which illustrates the crisis of the two chief systems of thought which divide mankind, the United States and the U.S.S.R. each possess an 'overkill capability'. They have more than enough bombs to wipe out humanity—surely one of the most extraordinary forms of waste of modern times.

I am well aware that in China, from where I have just returned as a matter of fact, the feeling is that the steady progress towards war is a good thing and that humanity will survive in the end, for since man created armaments he will always remain in control of those armaments.

It is a point of view which makes me shudder, I admit, and I think it is better to try to spare ourselves certain

1 Resolution 3281 adopted by the United Nations General Assembly at its 29th regular session on 12 December 1974 by 120 votes in favour, 6 against and 10 abstentions.

catastrophes while there is still time. Unhappily we see no
sign to make us think that the world is trying to slow the
arms race. On the contrary, nuclear expansion, nuclear
proliferation, has become one of the major problems of
government, and you cannot meet a head of state or a
minister of foreign affairs without his bringing the subject
up almost immediately. But mankind is not threatened by
arms alone: it is also threatened by scarcity. I am not one
of those who believe that the Club of Rome was entirely
right in forecasting total depletion. [2] I think somehow that
mankind in fact has enormous reserves available to it. But
it still has to discover them. And to do this, to exploit them,
we must be prepared to consent, in time, to enormous
investments. Everyone knows, however, that in the sphere
of energy, in particular, not enough effort has been made,
that consumption has not been sufficiently reduced, and
that as a result we find ourselves threatened before the
end of the century by a shortage which might have been
only relative but which is definitely liable to become
absolute.

Similarly, we are threatened by the contradiction between
insufficiently developed resources and our soaring population
figures. Without spectacular measures in the latter domain,
we are threatened with catastrophe there too.

In all spheres, I think, mankind is faced with the problem
of its very survival. It is tragic, when one has professional
responsibilities in communication, to witness the extreme
indifference of the vast majority of people, in any case in the
developed countries, to the importance of such problems.
It seems to me that only extremely forceful, extremely
simple ideas (for there is no forceful idea that is not simple)
are likely to be able to change the direction in which the
world is heading, to however small an extent, and to halting
its progress towards, if not the apocalypse, at least a return
to that law of the jungle which has unfortunately dominated
almost all of its history.

It seems to me that, in fact, effort must be channelled in
the direction of solidarity: which is why I do not think we
can dispense with some sort of emergency investment
planning on a world-wide scale [3] which would as quickly as
possible set up an absolute priority: to ensure for the
coming years production of a certain number of basic
commodities, whether industrial products, energy, or food-
stuffs, and at the same time to aim at distributing them
better. The difficulties which would be encountered by a
programme cast in such terms are enormous, even if, to
make it more popular, it were put into the vivid terms of a

2   *The Limits to Growth*, the
first Club of Rome report
(1972). Its pessimism was
to some extent qualified in
the second Club of Rome
report (1974): *Mankind at
the Turning Point* (see, for
example, Chapter 7,
'Tug-of-War for Scarce
Resources').

3   The idea for a world-wide
emergency investment plan
comes from Mr Mahbub
Ul-Haq, Director of the
World Bank's Policy
Planning and Programme
Department, Washington
D.C. It was proposed in
1976, at the Algiers confer-
ence, in the context of the
Reform of the International
Order Project.

new Marshall Plan [4] calculated to fire the imagination (for there is no denying that all this runs counter to short-sighted self-serving). Are not Western industrialists coming more and more to fear the invasion of our markets by industrial goods turned out at low cost in the Third World? Yet it is worth reminding people that the United States faced that same threat in 1947 when it launched the Marshall Plan. It did, after all, create producers, and it was thanks to the emergence of this new class of European producers, or rather the restoration of this class of European producers, that the world economy finally got under way again. I think that, today, there is no alternative to expanding the market, and since there is nothing that can be reduced to economics alone, and people's deepest motivations are not so much economic as moral, it seems to me—in all this solidarity should be the rallying-cry. A revolution in thinking? I think that we must also talk of a Moral Revolution. Man must cease to be as pitiless as often he is—since he is not always so—as well as indifferent to the misfortunes of others. Only awareness of a moral commitment to global solidarity can ward off the disaster which threatens us all. In meetings of this sort, it is fairly easy to agree about what ought to be done, but it is much harder to agree about the means of doing it. We should never separate ideas, or theory, from practice, and we are all aware of this. How to bring about this mental transformation, this moral revolution, which all of us desire whole-heartedly—that is the major problem facing us. For my own part, I think that such a transformation presupposes serious constraints. People still have to be persuaded to accept those constraints. But how is it to be done?

4 The Marshall Plan was named after General George Catlett Marshall and was conceived and propounded while he was Secretary of State (1947–50). The plan involved huge grants to various European and Mediterranean countries. Among them, for example, the Federal Republic of Germany was given the equivalent of $3,500 million in aid while Greece received over $2,000 million and France over $2,000 million. Czechoslovakia at first accepted the Marshall Plan offer and then rejected it under pressure from the U.S.S.R. There were, of course, 'strings' attached to the programme. The aid was granted within the general framework of the United States export programme. The countries receiving Marshall aid were obliged to spend their grants and credits in the purchase of American goods to be transported in American vessels. It was a boon to the American and European economies and it bound all countries to the United States in a clients–supplier relationship which has since undergone the refinement of the American-controlled multinationals.

Doing more with less

Han Suyin

I have learned a great deal from the authentic voice of the Third World through President Echeverría whose excellent phrase sticks in one's mind: '... the reconquest of historical initiative'. From André Fontaine we have had the catalogue of catastrophes and pessimism, a point of view which I consider Eurocentric. And we have had a marvellous and friendly duel within the scope of statistics concerning the increasing developmental gap between the haves and the have-nots, and the financial manipulations, which keep the hungry hungry and the weak weak and exploited. Mr Buckminster Fuller has given a fascinating account which shows the fallacy of all these statistics because they are politically conditioned to maintain ignorance by the entirely wrong conceptions and utilization of the resources of the world, the use itself belonging to a system which builds affluence on garbage, which promotes waste and extravagance and spoliation. I have come across something which I would like to add about the industrialization of the Third World on which there has been an enormous number of conferences. [1] The Lima declaration of 1975 stated that the Third World should account for at least 25 per cent of the world's industrial production by the year 2000, but industry itself was not defined nor was its gross or net output specified. In May 1976 a conference went further and declared that the Third World must achieve an 11 per cent annual growth rate to reach this 25 per cent output by the year 2000—25 per cent by that part of the world which accounts for 75 per cent of humanity and which has all the primary materials and resources necessary. These are, of course, improbable

[1] The Second General Conference of the United Nations Industrial Development Organizations was held from 12 to 26 March 1975 in Lima. It was followed by the United Nations Conference on Trade and Development (Nairobi, May 1976) and the Ministerial Conference of the Group of 77 (Manila, 21 January to 7 February 1977).

targets—myths and visions. So long as it is quite clear that technology is held back from those who most need it and that the monstrous injustice of terms of trade between the so-called developed and the developing countries is perpetuated. But I am not going to be pessimistic because I do not understand the word pessimism. Neither am I going to be an optimist because that does not mean anything. Today we are devoted to being scientific and science means reality. So I am going to discuss certain realities and, in first place, the necessary solidarity of humankind.

I would like to say that first of all I am afraid that there is at the moment enormous export or exchange of certain things which are going to the Third World and which in no way benefit it. This is increasing. It forms the most important part of the budget for a good many wealthy countries and this consists of armaments: the export of armaments, weaponry. The world is getting more and more full of weaponry and some countries of the Third World which are very poor devote vast amounts of money to buying weaponry. I do not think therefore that this augurs for the next twenty-three years anything but war—war on many levels, in many different ways, in short, many foci of war. And it is ridiculous, it would be dishonest, to say that with this accumulation of weaponry, we are not going to have war. It is ridiculous, therefore, not to see solidarity within the terms of this realistic situation. In Africa, there are at present bloody conflicts between nations of the Third World. Supplies of arms and weaponry are constant and daily, even by air. Are these purely local conflicts? In every case, to my mind, they are wars by proxy. If we investigate what they are, if we really look deeper, then we must not take the effect for the cause. We must look for the basic cause of this conflict. The thing that no one has mentioned, that people, even intellectuals, avoid mentioning, is that we are in a situation of real war, or rather no war no peace, a situation in which we have two so-called superpowers engaged in an enormous contention expressed in terms of a weapon proliferation so horrendous and so vile that it stuns the imagination and leaves all of us in a state of cataleptic idiocy. This is the greatest waste of all. This is the cause of everything that we have tried to discuss. And I am a little surprised that it has not been made obvious. Perhaps it is not very popular to make such statements but I must make them. And I say that, to my mind, this is the real war, this is the real problem, that there is tribalism in the minds of even technologically superb people who are still striving for something called power and domination, which is really the cause of catastrophe and war. And because of this vast conflict the world is unstable and to impute to the Third World the instability, when the first instability is the fact that we never know whether we are going to be nuclearized or not, is dishonest. Instability does not come from within the Third World: it is caused by this conflict and no other.

So therefore, unfortunately or fortunately, I do not see anything really working until we are prepared to tackle that situation head-on, or rather as intellectuals, to meet the real challenge which is to articulate the truth about the constant danger that we all live in. We often talk about demography and galloping population problems as a danger. Now look at it in the context of this constant threat of annihilation, of the fact that so much money, so much energy, so much intellect, so much of man's initiative is extravagantly devoted to lethal death and not to life. Is therefore bad to have a galloping population problem? Well, there are two ways of looking at it. Certainly to have a galloping demographic problem is to have a population that increases, causes poverty, but if there is a nuclear catastrophe, who is going to survive? The nation that produces the most children. And therefore it is ridiculous, on the one hand, and quite rightly, to work for family planning (and I have worked for family planning in China and in South-East Asia for twenty years), and, on the other hand, to have this menace hanging over the peoples of the world who can only survive by increasing their numbers. So therefore there is a paradox in this, and we cannot really settle this problem of demography unless we also remove the fear, which exists in certain African countries, of being too few and not too many.

There is also the matter which President Echeverría called to our attention: the scandal of aid, the scandal of the penury of aid. For instance, railways in Africa. Despite the vast professions of goodwill, the enormous amount of cash in circulation, money cannot be found for essential things. Here I regret that I must mention Chinese aid. I am not trying to make propaganda and I did not intend to discuss China but I am convinced that I should mention that in the case of aid, it is the Chinese who have shown initiative, something which perhaps other countries who profess to aid the Third World, should study attentively. The two superpowers had been asked to build a railway in Africa, and both had declined, saying it was too difficult. So the Chinese assumed the task. [2] And everybody spoke of Chinese imperialism, except the Africans who wanted that railway, and now the railway is built. And the railway was

2 The railway in question is the 1,860-kilometre link between Dar es Salaam in the United Republic of Tanzania and Lusaka in Zambia, with its 320 bridges, 26 tunnels, 2,239 water points and 93 stations. Work on it started in 1967 and was completed on 14 July 1976.

built and the Africans knew that it was build for them, and not in order to manipulate them or to create interdependence, because at the same time the railway was built as inexpensively as possible, so that the African countries would not have too great a debt to pay back. And the people who worked on that railway, the Chinese, worked and lived at the same level, adopted the same standard of living as the Africans. Perhaps those two points should be brought more to the attention of those who talk about aid. If a Third World country—China is poor—if a poor Third World country can show solidarity in trying to aid countries that really need help and in ways which they really need it, for their basic infrastructure and without an eye to profit, if China, with all the limitations of its own needs and poverty, can do this, why cannot others?

Therefore when we speak of solidarity I think we must put solidarity into the right perspective and put first things first, namely group solidarity, hence self-reliance. Now this principle of self-reliance is being better understood all the time by the Third World because it has been so often seduced and cheated by relying on others. To achieve self-sufficiency as much as possible implies the reorganization of internal systems, it implies sacrifices, and therefore the times before us are not going to be times of peace or eulogy. They are going to be times of great and increasing breakups, realignment and upheaval, but through these there will be increased awareness of the peoples of the world. By the year 2000, therefore, I feel optimistic in predicting reversal not of affluence as we know it now, but new realignments and a new consciousness of what is important and what is not important. And I think that by that time demography will also have played its role. I am thinking of a country I visited last year, namely Australia, where, due to the efforts of the Club of Rome, the population growth had, I was informed, dropped to zero. With only 13 million people in an area as vast as China, the Australians still consider themselves too numerous. I think that the real danger for the industrialized and wealthy world is senescence and senility, in the next twenty years there will be many old people. And that is why I am not optimistic about sudden change of heart in rich countries. On the contrary I think that they will cling more and more to their affluence and need more and more comforts proper to old age. But this is going to produce a reversal that will not bring an end to the Third World's problems but only a real awareness of these problems. Therefore I think that the role of the intellectual today is to know this reality which is unpalatable but which we must live with, just as we accept the indignity of what is called 'détente'. There can be no détente as long as arms escalation continues. There is a new generation of weapons coming out soon. The role of the intellectual is to state realities and to refuse to cheat people, even if this makes for unpopularity. It is only through this refusal to accept the slavery implied in the situation today that there is, I think, any hope. And I think the time will come when every liberal intellectual—and I am not talking politics, because I myself am not a Marxist—will have to stand up and be counted, and no longer simply take refuge in words. This is all I want to say. I believe in self-reliance. I believe in man. I think we are going to make it. I think that in my travels throughout the Third World countries, I have seen the hope of the world. Not the hope of emulating this distorted affluence that you have here, but the real hope of a more human world. But I do not hold out any hope that it will come easily. I do not hold out any hope that people who are unwise today will suddenly be wise tomorrow, either through morality or through enlightened self-interest which is the same thing. Not that there is no hope of understanding. This Round Table is indeed a shining example of the awareness, even in rich and industrial countries, of what is wrong. Even in certain industrial countries there is a great uneasiness about the policies that are being pursued, and although I hold out very little hope that they will be changed, I am gratified to be able to mention it. There is, for instance, Japan. Now Japan is a highly industrialized country and yet in Japan today there are a great many questions being asked and if you want to read about them, I would recommend *Foreign Policy* [3] written, I think, by some Americans and Japanese. There will be solidarity and there is solidarity and collective prosperity, but it will have to be fought for. There are clear and simple ideas that are being put into practice in China, for instance, and I am gratified to say that in 1956, the Chinese were already thinking in terms of the year 2000. Economy, frugality, hard work—thinking in terms of generations and not only the individual. These are the moral infrastructures necessary for clear thinking whether it be in technology, science or politics.

3 *Foreign Policy*, a quarterly published by National Affairs, Inc., New York.

Brainwashing with a good clean bomb

Sean MacBride

It is well to look back since we last met [1] and weigh the steps forward or backwards that humanity has taken.

The only gleams of hope that I have been able to observe recently are two: first of all, the advent of a United States President who has declared himself committed to the abolition of all nuclear weapons; second, the increasing commitment by Leonid Brezhnev, Secretary-General of the Communist Party of the Soviet Union, to the achievement of détente despite all obstacles.

However, so far these two psychological factors have not been matched by any concrete measures of disarmament. On the contrary, the arsenals of nuclear weapons and delivery systems have increased substantially. More significant still is the fact that, while there have been some abortive talks of partial measures of arms control and of the possibility of another Test Ban Treaty, there has been absolutely no mention of general and complete disarmament. In the light of the existing armament situation in the world, where twenty times more nuclear weapons are deployed than are necessary to destroy the entire human race, test ban treaties and other partial measures are utterly irrelevant.

As far back as 1961,[2] the then leaders of our world had agreed that humanity faced self-destruction unless all nuclear weapons were outlawed and unless general and complete disarmament was achieved. This was solemnly declared in 1961. It was decided upon by the then leaders of our world and their chosen experts: leaders and experts who had lived through the last war. We are told now that general and complete disarmament is not a realistic policy.

1   At the Round Table on Cultural and Intellectual Co-operation and the New International Economic Order, organized by Unesco (23–25 June 1976), Sean MacBride stated that 'there is an urgent need for a complete readjustment of our standards of public and private morality...'

2   A reference to the Kennedy–Khrushchev meeting in Vienna, Austria, from 2 to 4 June 1961, after which Mr Salinger and Mr Kharlamov released a joint communiqué: 'President Kennedy and Premier Khrushchev have concluded two days of useful meetings during which they have reviewed the relationships between the United States and the Soviet Union as well as other questions that are of interest to the two States. Today (June 4), accompanied by their advisers, they discussed the problems of nuclear testing, disarmament ...'. The advisers included Mr Rusk and Mr Llewellyn Thompson on the United States side and Mr Gromyko

Does that imply that the leaders and experts from 1945 to 1961 were irresponsible fools, or, is it that the leaders of today are not facing up to the realities that confront us? Why have the agreements of 1961 been shelved? Why are they never even mentioned now?

In the past year there have been some frightening new developments in addition to the very substantial increase in world armament. One State, South Africa, is on the verge of becoming a nuclear power with technological help and equipment furnished, in part at least, by States that claim they do not want to see any other States acquiring nuclear capacity. The advent of South Africa as a nuclear power poses a threat, not only to the African continent but to all the nations, and in particular to those of the Indian Ocean. It is surely hypocritical and meaningless to discuss a 'Zone of Peace' in the Indian Ocean if South Africa is going to dominate the Indian Ocean with nuclear weapons from Simonstown or from Valindaba, its nuclear centre.

The American Committee for Economic Development, [3] since we last met, published an important research paper on nuclear energy and national security. In this report it stated:

In 20 years, 100 countries will possess the raw material and the knowledge necessary to produce nuclear bombs. By the year 2000, the total plutonium produced as a by-product of global nuclear power will be the equivalent of one million atomic bombs. This is an alarming prospect. There is no straightforward military protection against these forthcoming dangers nor is there any foreign or commercial policy that can arrest the development of the capability to construct nuclear weapons.

Leaving that aspect aside let us examine what the 'alienated militarists' have been doing recently. They have discovered a new nuclear warhead which is cheaper to make and more effective. It is called the neutron warhead. It kills a greater number of people by radiation than the conventional nuclear warhead, but it spares the buildings and other property. A recent issue of the *Washington Post* put it this way: 'What the military friends of the neutron warhead admire so ardently about it, is its primary effect of killing people, and killing them in a clean way, by radiation rather than blast and heat.'

But this is only one of the new nuclear engines intended to destroy the human race upon which our 'alienated militarists' are working. In the last few weeks armament experts have told me that a new ultrasonic bomb has now been perfected which destabilizes the human brain and which can render the whole population of a city imbecile. By

and Mr Menshikov on the Soviet Union side, the latter being the then Ambassador to Washington. The nuclear test ban treaty was signed in Moscow on 5 August 1963 by the United States, the United Kingdom and the U.S.S.R.

3 The American Council for Economic Development (CED), founded in 1942, is not a State body. It brings together businessmen and economists, carries out research on major economic problems—in particular, full employment and higher living standards—and publishes special studies.

destroying certain cells in the brain, it converts human beings into raving idiots incapable of reasoning or of controlling themselves; and this is an irreversible process. It also does so without damaging property. It is a most desirable weapon because it does not destroy buildings nor does it spread radiation. It is also much more humane as it does not kill, it merely converts human beings into animals or vegetables.

I shall mention one other gruesome matter to illustrate the depth to which our 'alienated militarists' and scientists have sunk. There appeared four months ago a small news report which received little or no attention on this side of the Atlantic. It announced that the Pentagon had imported 45,000 frozen human foetuses from abortions in the Republic of Korea. It was explained that these frozen foetuses were necessary to test the effectiveness of radiation on freshly frozen human tissues. Human tissues from corpses were not adequate. These are the people whom we are employing —and whom the taxpayers of the world are paying—to do this kind of work.

The events which I have mentioned are but further evidence of the breakdown of morality in the world. The science-fiction revolution which has overtaken humanity since the last war has not been matched by the development of a counterbalancing sense of moral responsibility. I feel that we have not adequately dealt with aspect of the problem in the course of our discussions. There is no doubt that we can avert the destruction of humanity; there is no doubt that if we devote our attention to peace and not war we can prevent humanity from destroying itself. But this depends upon the willingness of our governments to do so, upon their desire to do so. It depends upon there being a moral conscience among the leaders of the world that will insist upon peace and not war as their uncompromising priority.

Albert Schweitzer [4] warned us thirty years ago that man had lost the capacity to foresee and forestall the consequences of his own inventiveness. This is only too true, but in the course of these thirty years moral standards have fallen and there has been a total breakdown in public morality. Science, unaccompanied by wisdom based on moral and ethical responsibility, has in itself become a threat to human survival. Wisdom in this context means a realization that the universe was not created by man and that man, by tampering with nature, is endangering the survival of the human species. Moral responsibility in this context means an ethical belief in the duty of human beings to help each other to survive and to share the goodness and beauty of the world which

4 Albert Schweitzer (1875–1965), French theologian and medical missionary, founded a hospital and a leper colony at Lambaréné in Gabon. Was awarded the Nobel Peace Prize in 1952.

providence has placed at the disposal of humanity. While this may sound religious it is essentially the same doctrine as that which is preached by Communism; in brief, it is a question of sharing the resources of the world and utilizing them for the benefit of humanity.

It is disastrous that at a time of complete moral decadence, certainly in the Western world, man should have acquired the ability to destroy all life on this planet.

One of the troubling aspects of this whole situation is the tendency of our political leaders and our mass media to underplay the arms race and its impact on the survival of humanity. Is this semi-silence accidental or is the question too awesome? Or again, are the military and armament lobbies effectively silencing the mass media and the press? The only way in which the folly of the arms race can be stopped is by the development of mass public opinion that will not allow governments to spend the major resources of the world in promoting a nuclear world war, that will accept nothing less than world disarmament.

This brings me to one urgent problem about which something could and should be done. If it is true that an informed world public opinion is the main safeguard against a nuclear war, then it is obvious that the press and the mass media are of vital importance. But unfortunately we seem to be living in a period in which the press and the mass media are also facing tremendous economic and political pressures. In some areas of the Western world, multinational and economic interests closely linked to the industrial–military complexes are striving to acquire and dominate important organs of the press. In Britain, the *Observer*, which has a long respectable tradition, has now been acquired by an American oil company.[5] In another case, an unconscionable multinational company, aptly described by a British Tory Prime Minister[6] as 'the unacceptable face of capitalism', is in the process of trying to acquire other important organs of the British press, as it has already done in Africa. In France, we have just witnessed the Hersant–Figaro troubles.[7] In Germany we have the Springer press affair.[8] In Italy we know of the control exerted by Fiat over the press.[9] We also know that government-controlled mass media in Britain and France have not allowed certain films such as *The War Game*[10] to be shown.

Has the time not come when some body, possibly Unesco, might undertake the examination of this problem and propound a draft declaration or even a draft convention to secure the right to freedom of information? This is necessary to ensure that public opinion can be informed

5 The company concerned is Atlantic Richfield.

6 Edward Heath.

7 The Hersant Group directly controls twelve French dailies (including two Paris papers, *Le Figaro* and *France-Soir*) and also takes in a fortnightly periodical (*L'Auto-Journal*), nine local weeklies and eleven specialized monthly publications. The purchase of *Le Figaro* in 1975 and the control exercised by Robert Hersant despite resolute opposition from the editorial staff led to the resignation of some of the *Figaro*'s journalists.

8 Springer controls 28 per cent of the daily press (including two Sunday newspapers) and two television magazines (14 per cent of the market).

9 Fiat owns *La Stampa* (Turin).

10 *The War Game*, a British film produced by Peter Watkins in 1966 on the theme of the nuclear destruction of an English village. The film was not widely distributed.

objectively as to what is happening in the world and how our very existence is threatened. Possibly, if Unesco is not in a position to undertake this task by reason of its varied political composition, this question might be examined by the Council of Europe, as far as Western Europe is concerned. A convention analogous to the European Convention on Human Rights [11] might well be considered in regard to the press. Such a convention should provide for the investigation of individual complaints and should be empowered to inquire into attempts being made to manipulate the press or the mass media, or to minimize the dangers that face humanity as a result of the policies pursued by governments.

I know that this is not a matter which we can examine here but I mention it in the hope that either Unesco or the Council of Europe will deal further with this urgent problem. It is important to create public opinion. It is also essential to ensure that we are not manipulated by governments, by the industrial–military complex, or by other economic interests that favour armaments or war.

11 The European Convention on Human Rights, signed at Rome on 4 November 1950, entered into effect on 3 September 1953.

The murky maze of indebtedness

Janez Stanovnik

I would like to discuss the rather alarming subject of indebtedness in the world. What has actually happened? Before the so-called oil crisis, we had on the average about a $20,000 million annual deficit in the world which occurred from year to year almost invariably on the side of the developing countries. Only after the oil crisis began, did the situation start changing, but it is rather interesting to see in exactly what way. Due to the increase of oil prices, there was an annual transfer from the oil-importing to the oil-exporting countries of, I will say, $100,000 million. It is extremely interesting to note that we, the developed countries, kept on arguing for two decades that any massive international transfer to the developing countries was impossible, that this was economically and technically unfeasible. Now from the moment OPEC [1] countries fixed prices, suddenly it became possible. What was earlier impossible, the transfer of $100,000 million, altogether in a year became possible. Now, what is extremely interesting to me is that this $100,000 million which went to the oil-exporting countries was then recorded as a deficit, not of $100,000 million, but of $150,000 million. This is a mystery to me. Shortly after the oil crisis began, the deficit of both developed and developing oil-importing countries was bigger than the oil bill. Now I would like to offer some explanation at this point. What happened? The oil-exporting countries did not have at their disposal a world banking network to manage this money. Therefore, this massive quantity of financial resources was recycled via the existing banking mechanism in European countries and in North America. This recycling

1 OPEC (Organization of Petroleum Exporting Countries) was set up in September 1960 in Baghdad, Iraq. Its statutes were approved in January 1961 in Caracas, Venezuela. In 1977, the OPEC member countries were: in Africa—Algeria, Gabon, Libyan Arab Jamahiriya, Nigeria; in Latin America—Ecuador, Venezuela; in Asia—Indonesia, Iran, Iraq, Kuwait, Qatar, Saudi Arabia, United Arab Emirates.

operation, though, was entirely private and therefore the accumulated funds, close to $200,000 million, were largely provided by private banking sources.

Now this is the point which interests me most of all. Why did the private bankers, who in my view have probably a better instinct for what is profitable in the long run and what is safe and what is not safe, than bureaucrats do—why did the private bankers lend money to developing countries who for more than two decades were considered to have but meagre development potentialities? The fact is the moment private bankers had the money, they invested it in various countries such as Mexico, Brazil, Nigeria and Indonesia. I see in this a clear indication that business people do have confidence in the economic future of these countries. They know the developmental potentiality of these countries even though officially the potentialities of the entire developing world were on the whole very poor. Let me go then a step further. Why did private bankers send money into the centrally planned socialist economies? Nobody could convince me that it is because they are ideologically closer to the communist countries than the official governments of the West are. The reason was very simple. Realistically, they deemed that the credit-worthiness of countries where the government controls the economy was greater than the others. Now I come to my real argument. I think that the calculation of these private bankers was in the long run correct. They said private firms might go bankrupt but States and countries never, and neither the community of developed countries nor the governments of developed countries could permit the entire financial system to collapse. And I think that it was on this assumption that the private bankers safely recycled the money into countries with an economic future, knowing that even if these countries were caught in a foreign-exchange squeeze or were unable to export as much as was needed to repay their debts, there would always be the governments of the developed countries to run the risk of assuming responsibility for these debts in the knowledge that Mexico, Brazil, Nigeria, Indonesia, etc., simply would not nor could not go bankrupt. Hence my optimistic conclusion.

I think the private bankers have indicated that the theory that the developing countries have meagre and poor prospects for economic development is quite simply not true. Actually, as soon as it appeared possible, the private bankers started investing in the developing countries rather than getting involved in the deficit of the developed countries, and this contradictory situation actually points to the reality, a long-hidden reality, whose truth was not known. Private bankers have shown the way to world development. The developed countries can no longer simply keep to themselves. They must, as it were, connect with the rest of the world.

There is another question to which I indirectly referred earlier. If you look at the developed countries you will see that the cumulative deficits in those countries increased after the oil crisis. Why? Because the developed countries refused to adapt to the new situation. The United States turned up last year with a deficit of approximately $11,000 million whereas it had shown a slight surplus the year before. Now this deficit almost exclusively came under the heading of oil. If you look at the oil bill of the United States, you will see that last year it amounted to $35,000 million—an increase explained by the refusal of the developed countries to conserve energy. There is a great deal of talk about the need to conserve energy but nobody does anything about it. And when I plead for a new life-style this is what I mean. We cannot go on wasting resources, wasting scarce and non-renewable resources in this way, on the false premise that there are finances available currently to acquire unlimited amounts by recycling the surpluses accumulated by the oil-exporting countries. In other words, why should the limits be exceeded simply because there is money available? I think this is a matter deserving of serious consideration especially where the developed countries are concerned. It is intolerable in the long run for the developed countries to maintain deficits in their balance of payments simply because they know that finances are available painlessly. Sooner or later, the developed countries will have to take severe measures to balance consumption with their ability to pay.

Countries, like individuals, are motivated by self-interest but they have to learn to recognize what is in their interest and how best to protect it . The advantage of a Round Table discussion like the present one is to show how an international organization like Unesco can educate people and show them what is in their interest. The true purpose of education and science is to prepare the future and to instruct man as to his real interests. Once he knows he can change his behaviour accordingly. This is what justifies my optimism.

When money cannot cure poverty

Paul-Marc Henry

The attitude of the private bankers towards the developing countries has in fact been much more favourable than might have been expected. But I should like to draw attention to the fact that their decision to grant loans is not always based on what they judge to be these countries' potential for enrichment and development. Here too 'enlightened self-interest' comes into play, for I imagine it is fairly profitable to be engaged in the three- and seven-year Eurodollar market with the London indexed rate at 7.5 to 8.5 per cent. In my opinion, the receipts of the private sector are at present due essentially to the world cash flow situation. The enormous amounts of money involved explain why private banks are interested in this kind of financing. Another reason why these loans have been made is that, at least from the point of view of the developing countries, there have been 'no questions asked'. The credit rating of a country like Zaire, for example, has been broadly assessed on the basis of copper production—copper production at a certain price. This was an error, incidentally, for the price of copper collapsed two years ago. Hence the present crisis. But in such cases decisions have always been based on current market showings, not on the amount of structural investment designed to bring about real change. It would be interesting, too, to know what proportion of this kind of financing is spent on immediate consumption. Let me remind you that the recycling of the famous $100,000 million is not a recycling directed towards investment and saving, but a recycling directed towards consumption: money spent on oil is consumption, not saving. Saving is deferred consumption, not accelerated consumption.

What we have here, therefore, is not at all the sort of long-term investment typical of the end of the nineteenth and the beginning of the twentieth centuries, which gave the world its first phase of development and its first infra-structural integration through transport, railways, ports and maritime communications.

The world virtually opened up between 1860 and 1914, but the money invested then, invested for fifty years and bringing in a gold-indexed interest of between 3.5 and 4.5 per cent, came from genuine savings (consumption being lower than income) on the part of the working masses in Europe (investment in Russia, for example, was financed to a considerable extent by the savings of ordinary people in France). There is a false impression abroad that there has never been so much money available for investment as there is now. But this money is not really being devoted to productive investment, but to the acceleration of consumption. If we look at the situation in the developing countries —with the possible exception of Brazil, and perhaps of India—the amount of work being done on infrastructure is very limited. For example, there are no big programmes for building railways. There is one very important Afghan project for building a railway to link Afghanistan with Iran—it is going to cost about $4,000 million but it is impossible to find those $4,000 million needed to finance it.

A second, very important and very alarming, point is that, because of the ease of short-term financing, the pro-portion of income to be devoted to repayment of debts is in some countries steadily increasing. A recent figure for Egypt, for instance, shows that 32 per cent of foreign income must be devoted to servicing debts.

So one must add that 32 per cent. What is even more serious is that more and more convertible currency is going into the purchase of food products.

There are certain countries, which shall be nameless, at present in full industrial expansion as regards the production of gas, and where 40 per cent of the imports are food products.

If you add the cumulative effect of short-term debts to the burden of Euro-payment on the balance of payment, the deficit comes at present to some $30,000 million. But behind this figure lies a condition of extremely serious social dete-rioration in the countries concerned. (This is not true of the socialist countries—they have their infrastructures, they are in a phase of full industrial expansion, and their gross rate of industrial growth is between 7 and 8 per cent, 9 per cent in some cases, which is almost comparable with Japan.) But in the developing countries I can see no growth in production that is at all proportional to their borrowings. In other words, borrowing acts as an accelerator to consumption, and thus perpetuates social differences within these countries by giving a certain caste access to Western-type consumption while the people at large sink into ever-greater poverty. It seems to me that the present careless attitude to the problem of debts is a manifestation of our profound ignorance of the real situations obtaining in these countries.

They are deteriorating. The poverty is linked to debt, and debt is linked to poverty. Many of the food debts are due to massive imports of food products to feed capital cities overcrowded with an influx of people from rural areas which are no longer productive. In other words, debt has become the reflection of a structural imbalance plus artificial consumption.

I think that, some day or other, there will be a straightening out of this situation. There will be a moment, or a year, of truth. And it will be painful, as it was in 1936 and 1937. There has been talk of a New Deal. I do not want to quarrel with my friend Stanovnik, but it is a question of history: the New Deal was introduced in 1933, but as you know the American depression started up again worse than ever in 1940, and in 1941 there came the war.

That was the great adjustment. And what I am afraid of is a repetition. It may seem momentarily encouraging and agreable, like the effects of drugs or alcohol, to see these changes going on before our eyes. Afterwards, however, comes the hangover, and we are heading for one gigantic economic hangover.

As for the problem of employment (and without employment I believe there can be no future), we are almost certain —it was discussed at Geneva—that, in order to give employment to the world's young people, we need to create some 350 million jobs in the next ten years. If we allow a minimum of $20,000 capital investment as the cost of creating one job, we begin to see the size of the problem. And I think this problem of youth is the absolute key to the whole matter. But—and this is the whole point of my contribution—the tendency of our technology is to reduce the number of jobs. It is no use trying to put the clock back and create a centralized economy. That is all very fine, but if, at the same time, advanced technology is destroying the social texture and the possibilities of employment—whether in industry, where there are fewer and fewer jobs available for young people, or in agriculture, where there is now no room for young people, or in commerce, where supermarkets are displacing many less-concentrated forms of trading (I am speaking here, of course, of our own societies)—then it is obvious that, even if we do wish to reverse our direction, the fatal machine which destroys employment has been set in motion.

It is already in motion in all the Western countries, which is why the OECD recently decided to hold a conference on employment. In the developing countries, the tragedy is total and absolute: in some, unemployment, calculated on the most conservative definition, affects from 30 to 40 per cent of young people. And no one has yet found a way to give these youngsters any sort of work. Do not believe those who say that the young people will go back to the country-side. They will not. It would be directly contrary to the principle of increased productivity in agriculture. They might indeed be returned—but only under conditions which have nothing to with freedom.

I do not like to end on this note, but I must, all the same, bring up this problem. Here we have, clearly, a generation which is out of work. And we may well find that unemployment among the young leads to militarization and terrorism. The average age of a terrorist is 22. The war in the Lebanon was fought by young militants aged between 16 and 20. The average age of the Khmer Rouge is under 20. Those are the grim facts. And there I think is the essential problem which overshadows everything else. If our élitist society were to be submerged by a younger generation for whom it has no use, if it were to trouble itself only about its own survival, well, that would be a real case of collective suicide.

The well-meaning technologists

Alfred Kastler

At this Round Table, gathered to study on a world scale the challenge of the year 2000, I find myself obliged once more to play the part of Cassandra. This is not because I am deliberately pessimistic. But even if one is optimistic I think it is both necessary and salutary to define the dangers, for only if people perceive them clearly can they organize appropriate measures to avert them. Those measures must be taken on a supranational level, on a world-wide scale, within the context of the United Nations.

To demonstrate this necessity, I have chosen to speak on two themes connected with what is now called 'ecology', i.e. the relationship between man and nature. The two subjects I propose to examine serve to show the extent to which the human race can interfere with natural conditions and alter climates on a world scale: I am going to speak of the evolution of the world's great forests and of pollution of the surface of the oceans.

I take my data on forests from a book by a distinguished expert, Roger Heim,[1] my colleague at the Académie des Sciences and Professor Emeritus of Botany at the French Natural History Museum. He sounded the alarm in 1973, when he published *L'Angoisse de l'An 2000* (The Fear of the Year 2000). He has sailed all the world's seas, and visited every continent.

In prehistoric times, when the representatives of the human species were still few in the world, a large proportion of the land which had emerged from the sea was covered with forests. The forest plays an essential part in the world's climatic equilibrium. The process of photosynthesis per-

[1] Roger Heim, a French scientist and member of the Institut de France, has done a great deal of work on mycology, tropical pathology and the protection of nature. His books include *La Sombre Route* (The Dark Road), 1945 and *L'Angoisse de l'An 2000*, published in 1973 by the Singer Polignac Foundation, Paris.

formed by green plants, changes the carbon dioxide in the atmosphere into oxygen. A large part of the oxygen in the atmosphere originates in this biological process, and oxygen is indispensable for animals to breathe. But the forest and its undergrowth also play an essential role in the world's hydrological equilibrium. The forest retains rain-water, releasing it only gradually into the streams and rivers. In this way it regulates the world's climates, helping to even out the rain chronologically. Without the forests, rain patterns would be much more jagged and periods of drought would alternate with floods, both equally destructive.

From time immemorial, man has been a destroyer of forests. We know that, in prehistoric times, the shores of the Mediterranean, both in Europe and in Africa, were covered with forests. Fossilized wood has been found in what is now the Sahara Desert. In antiquity and throughout the Middle Ages, man, together with his formidable companions, sheep and goats, succeeded in 'desertifying' Spain, the south of France, southern Italy, Greece and the African coastlands. A recent example of this effect of human activity is the disappearance of the famous cedars of Lebanon forest which was decimated in the nineteenth century to provide fuel for Turkish locomotives plying between Istanbul and Cairo. The advent of the age of industrialization and colonization accelerated the process of destruction.

Heim quotes a typical example: Madagascar. In 1895, one-third of the island was still covered in forest: i.e. 20 million hectares out of a total area of nearly 60 million. According to the 1971 census there are now only 1.4 million hectares of forest left. In three-quarters of a century man has wiped out 93 per cent of the island's forests, and of the trees which still stood at the end of the last century only 7 per cent remain.

Events have followed a similar pattern in North Africa. Where in 1830 there were still 5 million hectares of forest, in 1953 only half were left. And it is no exaggeration to say that, in the last hundred years, man has managed to destroy half of the great virgin forest of equatorial Africa.

Natives and colonizers are equally guilty. To clear the land and make way for fields, the local inhabitants have no hesitation in setting fire to the forest. The timber trade and the need for massive production of cellulose for the paper industry are factors which complete the destruction. It is a platitude to say that one day's issue of the *New York Times* involves the sacrifice of several hectares of northern Canadian forest.

And now man has started on the last remaining great tropical forest, and has succeeded in crossing Amazonia with his bulldozers. It will not be long now before the forest is torn apart.[2]

In these circumstances, it is scarcely a matter for surprise if, even in France, we have more and more extreme alternations between drought and inundation; and if there is drought in the Sahel and catastrophic flooding in Bangladesh.[3] Of course there have always been climatic irregularities, years of fat kine followed by years of lean kine as in the Bible. But it cannot be denied that the phenomenon is growing more marked; and man's behaviour has something to do with it. Only too seldom do we hear of anything being done, as in Israel, to replant deserts with trees. Such examples ought to be imitated, for the best way of harnessing solar energy for terrestrial use is the method nature has used for millions of years—photosynthesis in plants.

And now for my second subject: the pollution of the surface of the oceans by what scientists call hydrocarbons and what is commonly known as oil.

According to the experts of the United Nations Environment Programme (UNEP), who met in Paris this past spring,[4] 6 million tons of oil are discharged every year into the world's seas. Two million are dumped by tankers cleaning out their tanks and other ships blowing off their boilers. The remaining 4 million come from coastal refineries, industrial waste washed down by rivers, accidents (for example, those of the *Torrey Canyon* and of the *Bohlen*),[5] and leaks from undersea fields like Ekofisk.[6] The sea has really become a dustbin for modern man.

According to Professor Pérès, Director of the oceanographic station at Endoume-Marseilles, the above-quoted figure needs to be at least doubled to allow for the unconsumed fuel from ships' funnels which is deposited on the sea. An annual figure of 10 million tons is probably a conservative estimate.

In an article in *Le Monde* of 5 April 1977 entitled 'La Mer Est Encore Capable de Digérer le Pétrole' (The Sea can Still Absorb More Oil), Madame Yvonne Rebeyrol says that all this pollution is negligible in proportion to the total volume of the seas all over the world, which is of the order of 1.4 thousand million cubic kilometres, i.e. roughly 10^{18} tonnes. The ratio between these masses, or volumes, of oil and water is equal to 10^{-11}; in other words the mass of oil discharged into the oceans every year is only one hundred-thousand-millionth of the mass of water. Should we then conclude, as the author of the article in *Le Monde*

2 Work on the trans-Amazonian highway (5,400 kilometres long) was begun some ten years ago. It will link Joao Pessoa, capital of the State of Paraiba (the most easterly part of Brazil) with the Peruvian frontier.

3 The Sahel was ravaged by drought in 1973 and 1974. The floods in Bangladesh took place in 1974.

4 UNEP held a specialist seminar from 29 March to 1 April 1977 on the effects of the oil industry on the environment. Taking part were some 250 experts of some 80 different nationalities.

5 *Torrey Canyon*, 1967; *Bohlen*, 1976

6 Ekofisk: the accident occurred in the spring of 1977 off the coast of Norway.

does, that ocean pollution is negligible? It would be quite wrong to do so. This is not a matter of the ratio between masses or volumes, but of the ratio between surfaces. To digress, if you will allow me, into a little lesson in physics: oil is made up of hydrocarbon molecules which are hydrophobic, i.e. insoluble in water. It remains concentrated on the surface of the water, and spreads there through gravitation. But this oil still contains from 5 to 10 per cent of oxydized molecules or organic detergents containing oxygen—what physicists call semi-absorbents—which penetrate into the water by means of their oxygen-bearing extremity, forming what is known as a mono-molecular layer on the surface of the sea. These layers have been intensively studied by the French physicist Henri Devaux[7] and the American physicist Irving Langmuir. Langmuir has shown that when oil contains from 5 to 10 per cent of semi-absorbent molecules, these molecules spread over the water in a very thin mono-molecular covering. Over this layer the rest of the oil, the hydrophobic molecules, then spread, so that the two levels together form what Langmuir calls a 'duplex layer' on the surface of the sea, its thickness being determined by the proportion of oxygen-bearing molecules.

If the proportion is 5 per cent, the duplex layer will be 400 ångströms thick. This is only twenty-five-thousandths of a millimetre—very little, but not negligible. This being so, it is easy to calculate that one cubic metre of oil can cover a surface of twenty square kilometres of water. The total surface of the world's seas is some 300 million square kilometres, so the 10 million tonnes of oil discharged into the sea every year are enough to cover a surface of 200 million square kilometres, in other words could cover two-thirds of the total ocean surface. A still unknown factor in the problem is how long such patches of oil last. Their existence has been reported several times, in particular by the Norwegian explorer Thor Heyerdahl, who led the *Kon-Tiki* expedition.[8]

Farmers often use thin layers of oil on pools or ponds, to reduce evaporation or kill mosquito larvae. On still water the oil layers last for several weeks. But layers of oil like this, even if they are less than a ten-thousandth of a millimetre thick, substantially affect the exchanges between the hydrosphere and the atmosphere. The atmospheric oxygen which marine animals need in order to breathe, dissolves more slowly in the sea water, and the speed of evaporation of the water is reduced. Now it is basically that speed of evaporation which regulates cloud and rain patterns over the world's continents. So this pollution we are talking about,

7   Henri Devaux, a French physicist. In 1904 he submitted a paper to the French Society of Physics on *The Critical Thickness of Solids and Liquids in Very Thin Layers.*

8   In 1947, Thor Heyerdahl set out for Polynesia on a pre-Inca Peruvian raft, to prove that this was the route followed by Indians of Peru, where Polynesian culture originated. Tiki is the name of a pre-Inca god.

at its present level, and at some future level if it is not stopped, may have an appreciable effect on climate. It must be brought to an end.

Several international conferences have been held on the problem, under the auspices of the United Nations: in Caracas in 1973, in Geneva in 1975, and in Paris in 1977.

The problem of ocean pollution, like that of the vanishing forests of the world, shows the vital and urgent necessity for setting up a world organization, an international authority with powers of enforcement, to protect the human race of the future, who will otherwise be the victims of our improvidence. No such body exists at the moment. One ought to be set up under the aegis of the United Nations.

I should like to close with a further quotation from the book I mentioned earlier, by Roger Heim:

There is no question that, if this state of affairs is not countered by means of information and propaganda, backed up by severe and properly applied legislative measures, the damage man is doing to natural environments will get rapidly worse. The ominous increase in world population, the ever-increasing destructive power of modern technical methods and equipment, and man's more and more overweening ambitions to bend nature to his own needs, constitute a great danger facing humanity today.

Solidarity with our successors

Jean d'Ormesson

It strikes me that the key word emerging from this gathering —and it is not a very cheerful word—is 'pessimism'. Those of us who are here are optimists, or we would not be meeting together like this, in Unesco, to discuss problems and try to find solutions. But I would suggest that this optimism operates against a background of pessimism. Mr Stanovnik went back to 1950. Let us try for a moment to imagine we are in 1850. We would certainly have been optimistic then. Of course, there would still have been difficulties to overcome and problems to solve. But a fundamental element of optimism would have been provided by scientific progress. Now, by a paradoxical reversal, that same element has become one making for pessimism. It cannot be denied that science is suspect.

There is no need to dwell on the greatest misgiving of all—the possibility of destroying the universe. Suffice it to say that the first dilemma we are faced with is the alternative between suicide and survival. For the first time in its history, mankind is contemplating its own suicide. Of course it has often contemplated its own death. We need only think of the terrors that preceded the year 1000, or all the other fears that have racked mankind unnecessarily.[1] Enea Silvio de Piccolomini, later Pope Pius II, for example, wrote a famous letter in which he predicted that modern weapons would bring the world to destruction.[2] But in those days such threats concerned only one part or another of world civilization. Now we are confronted with a fundamental phenomenon which, unfortunately, will always remain with us for the future, whatever measures are taken: we

1 '... In the middle of the tenth century and throughout the eleventh, we find definite proofs or marked traces of the belief in the end of the world; in the years just before, and during, A.D. 1000, there is none. The decisive moment itself seems to have left people unmoved.... History contains both rational and irrational elements. The first category includes structural phenomena, major political and economic groupings, and certain clearly marked movements of thought. The second category takes us into much less clearly defined areas of human life, areas much more difficult to analyse because affective values exist in the eternal twilight of instinct. It is as if two human races were at work simultaneously, in the same places, but following completely different paths. The last years of the tenth century, including the year 1000, and the early years of the eleventh century, produced the most vigorous architects of Western civilization, sound and clear-headed, full of thoughts both wide-ranging and definite, even

shall forever be faced by the possibility of the suicide of all mankind from within, global suicide. So, if the game is to go on at all, it is absolutely necessary to ensure that there is a fellowship among all living persons that will allow them to choose survival instead of suicide. Let us assume, then, not that mankind opts for suicide—when the game would be over—but that the choice made is survival. It would still be hypothetical, but not beyond the bounds of hope.

Assuming survival, again two great difficulties have to be faced. The first is the law of differential growth, according to which the rich grow richer and the poor grow poorer. In addition to this, there is also the law of limited growth —the impossibility of the perpetual development, which a few years ago seemed a certainty and now seems more like a myth. Perhaps we—especially those of us who belong to a world that is rich—are entering upon an age when our world will be poor.

The obvious references that spring to mind are oil and the Club of Rome. It seems to me that there are two aspects to this ending of development, especially as it affects the rich countries. First is the need, if disaster is to be averted, to set up increasingly comprehensive methods of distributing wealth. Second is the possibility, perhaps amenable to discussion, perhaps inevitable in the more or less distant future, that certain kinds of the world's wealth will be used up. What admits of no doubt is that the fellowship among the living which I have just mentioned as being needed to ensure mere survival is no longer enough: we are entering upon an era—new to humanity—in which there has to be a wider solidarity with our successors, too—a solidarity embracing more than those now living, whether rich or poor, and including those who will come after us—if the world is not to become exhausted and cease to exist.

It could be said that the Christian idea of one's 'neighbour' has taken on a new dimension: our 'neighbour' is perhaps as yet unborn. We have other 'neighbours' to come, and to them also our fellowship must extend.

There must therefore be a dual solidarity—first among the living, to avoid suicide and ensure survival as a start, and then to guarantee an equitable division of that survival, and second between the living and those yet to come. There remains the question whether the only basis for it is to be found in moral virtues or whether it is not really a matter of enlightened self-interest. It may be suggested that moral virtue is merely, in a sense, the expression of self-interest

if imbued with certain impossible dreams.... The year 1000 shows a strikingly contrasting picture. Though there is no actual text which allows us to affirm that in the more obscure strata of society it was a year agitated by fear of the end of the world, it was nevertheless a year dominated by fear—a vague, generalized fear. The fear was not strictly linked to chronology: it began before A.D. 1000 and persisted after it.... Perhaps it is useful to remember that an age or a society is not all of one piece, but comprises several layers of humanity, a kind of moral geology.' —Henry Focillon, *L'An Mil—le Problème des Terreurs* (The Year 1000— the Problem of Fear).

2 E. S. Piccolomini (1405–64) became Pope in 1458. He was an eminent scholar and intellectual, and the range of his works demonstrates the extent of his learning. He wrote a *Cosmography*, a *Treatise on the Education of Children*, a *History of the Bohemians*, and a *History of Europe in the Reign of the Emperor Frederick III*. He also left 452 letters dealing with the problems and concerns of his day.

viewed in the long term. Virtue would then consist simply
in seeing further ahead than others, and having a longer-
term understanding of the common good.

A new social contract

The present exploring the way of the future

Mircea Malitza

Although it has hardly begun to be regarded as an independent discipline—not more than ten years have passed since world literature started to be invaded by writings about the future—the investigation of the future has already had an eventful history. Rapid social and political changes (what use now are the atlases of the 1960s?); the exploits of science (a few years ago, did anyone imagine photographs being taken on Mars?); the performance of technical feats which not long back would have been regarded as crazy (such as the transferring of an Antarctic glacier to Saudi Arabia!); the pressure of mankind's great problems (how to satisfy the basic needs of 4,000 million people); the mulitude of demands to be met, and the flagrant disparities between different human societies—all these are prompting communities to examine carefully the path opening up before them and to define as accurately as possible their choices and their aims.

The debate reached a climax in 1972. The World Conference on the Environment, meeting in Stockholm, introduced a new word into the current vocabulary. An International Conference on futurology studies was held in Belgrade. And the Club of Rome published a disturbing book on 'the limits to growth'. But despite the undeniable conceptual advance made in 1972, the theoretical structure which came out of it has not succeeded in standing up to the cross-fire of events.

Many new concerns were introduced by the great debate on energy, on the raw materials without which the huge machines of industry would grind to a halt, on the worst unem-

ployment ever known, and on inflation. What is the point
of talking about the year 2000, people said, when we cannot
even prevent a thing as simple but as momentous as inflation?
The inflation which then ravaged many countries made many
people doubt the usefulness of long-term conjectures. What
good are such conjectures if our control over individual
economies is so uncertain that we cannot even check the
increase here and now in the cost of living?

While in 1972 anxiety about the erosion of nature and the
upsetting of ecological balances prevailed throughout the
world, discussions two years later centred on the natural
resources required by industry and the absolute necessity
of maintaining their availability. Motorists were once more
haunted by thoughts of petrol rather than of pollution from
exhaust fumes. During the last four years, the period with
which we are particularly concerned, there have been
important changes of emphasis, many prophecies have
proved unfounded, myths have been exploded and the field
of debate has shifted to the sphere of the real and the
practical. The main trends which have emerged are, briefly,
as follows.

From the tendential to the normative method

According to Herman Kahn [1] and his followers, the future is
situated at the end of a number of produced tendential curves,
starting out from the established facts of the past and the
present. To this school of thought, the future is a mere extrapolation. There is no need for objectives: goals will gradually
be clarified by themselves. Trends are more powerful than
man's intervention, and lead inexorably to certain struc-
turalizations of the future independent of our norms. All
Kahn's works in this field, including those devoted to the
development of France and Japan up to the year 2000, are
influenced by this hypothesis which explains both his technological optimism and his tendency to underestimate the
influence of change and the emergence of new values
different from those adopted by advanced industrial societies.

In contrast, present-day thinking gives priority to norms
and to a vision of the future, which modify the pattern of
phenomena and direct them towards fixed goals. (Romania,
with its programme for building a multiple socialist society
which defines fundamental objectives for 1990, is an example
of this normative approach.) For Marxists, the image of
the future society always acts as a guide to the social activity
required for exercising rational control over the course of
history. At present the balance has swung in favour of the

1 Herman Kahn, American
futurologist (Hudson
Institute, New York).
Author of *Thinking the
Unthinkable* (1964), *The
Year 2000* (in collaboration
with A. G. Wiener) (1967),
*The Emerging Japanese
Superstate* (1971).

normative school which seeks for the means required by the objectives fixed rather than the explorative school which seeks what is possible in terms of the means at our disposal.

From neutrality to open commitment

There was a flow of writings proclaiming the need to strip future research of all ideology, but we now find an increasing number of authors obliged to admit that a forward solution of the great problems facing us implies an attitude, a commitment, the endorsement of some idea. This is evident from the series of reports prepared for the Club of Rome. The first, *The Limits to Growth* (1972), was strictly technical, painting a sombre future based on the interaction between resources, industry, pollution, population and food, and completely neglecting the human factor, creativity and accepted values. A second report, by Professors Mesarovitch and Pestel, was called *Mankind at the Turning Point* (1975). While claiming to be neutral, it did take human choices and decisions into account. The reshaping of the international order (RIO) was the subject of the third report, written by Professor Jan Tinbergen, Nobel prizewinner in economics, who recognized the impossibility of approaching the overall problems of mankind without adopting some 'attitude'. His report says that:

Balanced management must aim simultaneously at waging an immediate battle against poverty and at safeguarding the interests of future generations through the legacy of a habitable planet. Both are predominantly political and not technical issues; both belong to attempts to shape a new international order.[2]

From speculative exercises to the recognition of real problems

A significant change of direction became evident in 1976, in Dubrovnik, at the Conference of the World Future Studies Federation, founded after the conference held in Bucharest in 1972. Its president, Professor Johan Galtung,[3] spoke of the transition from a study of the future obsessed with the fads of a consumer society and pretending to ignore economic motives, to a study of the future ready to confront fairly and squarely the real problems of development. Hitherto, said Professor Galtung, the future had seemed a mere speculative exercise suitable for developed countries, which saw only the subsidiary and noxious consequences of industrial activity, whereas for developing countries the problem was how to make up as quickly as possible for lost time and how

2 *Reshaping the International Order*, p. 33, 1976.

3 Johan Galtung is a member of the Scientific Council of SIPRI (Stockholm International Peace Research Institute).

to tackle the immediate tasks arising out of this aim. There is now quite clearly a veritable meshing of problems on a world scale, involving the responsibility and calling for the efforts of all. Its elements are basic to man's existence: food, water, oxygen, oceans, population, resources, science and technology, environment, the best application of human resources. All these are giving rise to an unprecedented series of world conferences sponsored by the United Nations and non-governmental seminars and Round Table discussions. Many centres and institutes are working out global models. The realist trend here is illustrated by the world economic model recently established by Leontief, another Nobel prizewinner, who narrows things down to essentials by showing the need for developing countries to allocate between 30 and 40 per cent of their income to investment. No serious futurological research can be carried out unless account is taken of the major problem of development which faces all societies, even those who have entertained the fleeting illusion that it can be arrested.

From the controversy over science and technology to the acknowledgement of their role as a driving force

At one time all the troubles afflicting mankind were supposed to be due to the destructive and disruptive effects of scientific and technological invention. But though we may criticize certain undesirable consequences of science, we need not deny the driving force exercised by science and every kind of knowledge necessary for innovation. Nor has the debate on science been useless, for researchers and technicians are now making a fresh start which takes into account the problems of human existence and the need to exploit new sources of energy, primarily solar energy. The old-style technocrats are turning over a new leaf, admitting, with Forrester,[4] that what has to be explored in the coming years are not 'physical boundaries' but social ones. The social and economic consequences of disarmament are once more being closely studied. A group of experts chosen by the Secretary-General of the United Nations and working under Professor Gheorghe Dolgu, Rector of the Academy of Economics in Bucharest, is preparing a report on the subject.[5]

The new international economic order

This is the powerful unifying concept which emerges from a mass of notions all struggling for predominance—a concept related to all the world's major preoccupations. My country,

4 Jay Forrester, of MIT, author of *World Dynamics* (1972), created the prototype model used by the Club of Rome.

5 *Economic and Social Consequences of the Arms Race and of Military Expenditure*, published by the Department of Political and Security Council Affairs, United Nations.

Romania, is one of the most active in trying to establish a new international economic order. It emphasizes the political aspect of the concept, which implies the setting up of international relations on the basis of new principles which Romania has long advocated.

The concept of a new economic and political international order has grown steadily. In January 1976, an international seminar was held in Geneva dealing with the social dimension of the new international order, and in June of the same year we met again at a Round Table held in Paris on the cultural aspects of the problem. History has not often seen a flow of ideas, claims and actions on such a scale, involving such wide-ranging groups of people, all aiming at changing old relationships based on inequality and economic and political inequity, and at replacing them with new structures designed to bring the various different degrees of development closer together and to close the chasms still dividing the post-colonial world.

These ideas, far from being exhausted, require us to devote the utmost effort to their elucidation. The laboratories where this work is really done are not—as might be thought—meetings or research centres, however important, but the places all over the world where practical experiments in development are being carried out. A proper exchange of views is absolutely indispensable, whether for arriving at a synthesis or for deciding on the best direction to follow. I myself would suggest the following as the main topics requiring elaboration:

First, the final ending of the false alternative between nature and development, formulated in extreme terms in 1972, when it was thought that industry and cities inevitably caused nature irreparable harm.

Second, the choice to be made between growth and distribution, a dilemma based on the belief that all economic progress is bound to result in social differentiation and increased inequality of distribution.

Third, the new solutions to be looked for in the matter of transferring technology—one of the world's most acute and urgent problems. The debate on 'intermediate technology', which tends to monopolize attention in the developing countries, is not yet over.

Fourth, the recognition of varied life-styles and cultures, and the right of each people to choose its own path, need to be complemented by a study of the common elements in the experience of all societies and the contribution of each to the world heritage.

Finally, further investigation is needed into the relation between a country's internal possibilities and what international co-operation has to offer. Some newly independent States on the threshold of development consider that their own 'internal strength' is best expressed by autarky, the closing of frontiers, and the rejection of international co-operation. But in fact a sound and rapid pace of development presupposes an open attitude to the outside world and full-time use of the advantages of co-operation. Similarly, the cardinal principle that every people has the right to work out its own decisions is not at variance with co-operation; on the contrary, co-operation is founded on and guaranteed by that very principle.

Changed criteria

Many of the ideas launched during the last ten years have undergone revision in the fire of debate. Some have even lost their gloss. Take, for example, 'the quality of life'. The concept implied that there was a certain level in the satisfaction of life's quantitative needs which, once attained, left no other preoccupation but quality. Now, however, priority is given to providing an indispensable minimum for the majority of mankind. Almost all futurology studies have taken as their starting-point the definition of a threshold which must be crossed in order to rescue the least-favoured strata of society from inadmissible poverty. This idea has been developed by Latin American researchers such as the Bariloche school in Argentina.[6] In addition to the minimum threshold, the idea has emerged that a ceiling should also be fixed for consumption, beyond which consumption becomes waste and provocation. This kind of study, which brings out the inequalities in consumption, has been chiefly pursued by the Scandinavian school (see the writings of Gunar Adler-Karlson[7] and the studies published by the Dag Hammarskjöld Foundation in Sweden or the new For a New Kind of Development centre.

These priority concepts, closer to mankind's real needs, have come to the fore at the same time as the rehabilitation of productive labour. Until 1973–74 sociological literature was largely dominated by the problems of leisure. There were countless seminars on the subject. But this problem is not a matter of priority. Our chief preoccupations do not include a hypermechanized society in which human intervention is largely symbolic and unproductive activity has to be organized in order to avoid neurosis. What is in the forefront is the need to provide employment (World Confer-

6 The Bariloche Foundation was set up to construct a world model to a certain extent in opposition to the Club of Rome. The Bariloche Report, *Catastrophe or New Society*, was published by the International Development Research Center (Canada). The director of the project was Amilcar O. Herrera; the Director of the foundation, Carlos Alberto Mallmann. The team is now disbanded and the foundation inactive.

7 Gunar Adler-Karlson is a Swedish specialist in social science, professor at the University of Roskilde in Denmark. The Swedish Government has a permanent futurology secretariat in Stockholm.

ence of the ILO, Geneva, 1976),[8] and other equally urgent requirements such as the need to achieve a proper harmony between physical and intellectual labour, and to include in every model of supreme values the idea of work as an indispensable part of life and of a complete human personality.

The facts have exploded the vision of a post-industrial consumer society, and those who invented it are now abandoning it. The consumer society has been bitterly denounced as a consecration of waste. Hedonist post-industrialism, the picture of a future with a superabundance of goods and leisure derived from miraculous techniques— these are seen to be empty dreams. Nowadays, scientific discussion of models of the world of the future accept the following as principal factors: the incompatibility between partial criteria of economic optimality and the vital needs of society; the need to respect the natural balance; and the recognition that economics has a cultural and social dimension (see the work of the Association Internationale Futuribles founded by Bertrand de Jouvenel).[9] As we see all the time, the problems of mankind have become so complex that, given the speed at which the world is changing, they cannot be solved merely by the free play of forces; that could lead to disaster. The only answer lies in considered action and a rational approach, translated into a programme and a plan.

New methods

Futurology offers the researcher new tasks unknown to specialized analytical investigation. Futurology is synthetic and involves dozens of disciplines. It is thus an inter- and pluridisciplinary study. We must learn to work with large sets of data which cannot be broken down into components; with factors governed by relationships forming a single whole; with systems. Various disciplines already teach us how to measure temperature, length or intervals of time. But how are we to evaluate centrality, interaction, degrees of connection; how to classify objects according to several criteria; how to appraise natural states of equilibrium and tell, for instance, when a lake is about to be struck by disaster? The future brings pressure to bear on mathematics and scientific thought. Models require more and more specialized apparatus and increasingly difficult and lengthy calculations. The possibility of rounding out economics with social considerations has brought the question of social indicators to the fore. Techniques of investigation vie with

8 See The report *World Employment Programme; Research in Retrospect and Prospect*, Geneva, World Conference of the ILO, 1976.

9 The Association Internationale Futuribles was founded in 1976 by Bertrand de Jouvenel, who has taken part in the work and research of many international authorities, such as the Institute for the Future (United States of America), and the Social Science Research Council (United Kingdom). His publications include: *The Pure Theory of Politics* (1963), *L'Art de la Conjecture: Futuribles* (1964), *Arcadie: Essais sur le Mieux Vivre* (1968), *Du Pouvoir: Histoire Naturelle de sa Croissance* (Of Government: the Natural History of Growth) (1972), *La Civilisation de Puissance* (Power-based Civilization) (1976), and *Les Origines de l'Etat Moderne* (The Origins of the Modern State) (1976).

one another. They are real weapons for mastering complexity and controlling the models of the future. They are already helping with the solution of some complex problems, such as the development of river basins, town planning, and the organization of transport, factories, schools and other institutions.

The age of complexity

The characteristic feature of the period we have to live through until the year 2000 is not the accelerated speed and rhythm of events on which Alvin Toffler centres his book *Future Shock* (1970), but rather the growth of complexity.

For hundreds of years, the problems societies have had to solve have been relatively simple. After Descartes all complexity was reduced to its simplest expression. Our reason invented adequate instruments of analysis for itself, science became specialized, culture compartmentalized. And now suddenly we are confronted with extremely intricate problems—whether their intricacy arises from the number of factors involved, their degree of dependence or the growth of ambiguity, vagueness and uncertainty—while at the same time we are immensely eager to master the whole and comprehend the unity of reality.

We are thus at a parting of ways: either, overwhelmed by our inability to escape our own limitations, by the hesitations of reason when faced with complexity, we throw reason and reality, science and history, overboard, as the reactionaries of despair have done in every crucial period; or else we take reason and reality, science and history, as the starting-point of a determined and ambitious programme of innovation.

It would be wrong to allow the first defeatist trend to usurp the title of 'new philosophy'. I am appalled at the amount of attention paid to writers marked by a worn-out spirituality, and above all by the fact that they are wrongly labelled 'new'. There will be a new philosophy between now and the year 2000, but it will be based on the progress made by science in its efforts to master complexity, to dispel ambiguity in language and communication and to perfect different kinds of polyvalent logic and make them operational, so that, free from the tyranny of the old logic, we can make decisions even in conditions of uncertainty and move forward in the field of systems studies and techniques of synthesis. This possibility is not only very likely to come true: it is already, via characteristically discreet, anonymous and persevering efforts, achieving results.

Everyone agrees that we are still going through a revolution in technology and science, based on cybernetics and the theory concerning informational energy and control mechanisms acting ismorphically in man, society and man-made machines.

The natural consequence of this is a revolution in the intellectual instruments at our disposal for representing subtler, more complex and more profound processes which have eluded our previous approximations. My only note of caution here, and it is shared by many other scientists, derives not from any doubt about this revolution itself, but from the fear that there may be many people, even in intellectual professions, ill-prepared to understand and assimilate it. It will be greeted by cultures encumbered with prejudice and myth, their energies divided among the shrines of various Molochs, chief among them the arms race and the pursuit of new methods of destruction. That is why I believe that, if the end of our twentieth century is to be safe from upheaval and crisis, great efforts must be made on an unprecedented scale to educate people for the future. Such education is entirely different from organic and adaptive education, so dearly paid for and so fraught with risk. Education for the future is based on a rational model, on an attempt to forestall experience instead of actually undergoing it with all the harsh and costly lessons it brings in its train.

The lessons of experience

Vladimir S. Kemenov

The question 'What lies in store for mankind in the year 2000?' has already given rise to an enormous number of publications, scientific, philosophical, sociological and literary. Behind them all are the anxiety and uncertainty rife in the world.

According to Alvin Toffler this is a sort of malady, which he calls 'future shock', a kind of collision involving man and nature. But there is no scientific foundation for such a thesis. Karl Marx wrote:

We recognize only one science, the science of history. History may be examined from both sides, it may be divided up into the history of nature and the history of man. But both parts will be closely interconnected so long as man exists; the history of nature and the history of man condition one another.

The truth of those words is more clearly demonstrated now than ever. It is true that man may wipe out his own species if he does not do away with the risks of nuclear war and achieve total and final disarmament. But men want to live and survive—that is the first challenge. Disarmament would set free enormous sums to be used for culture, education and aid to developing countries. If industrial waste goes on increasing the pollution of our natural environment, the air, the soil, the seas, the rivers, the forests and the fields will bring sickness and death to every living thing, and the bell that rings in the year 2000 will be man's knell.

The unity of the world has become a fact, and the problems humanity has to solve are global. The relationship between man and nature no longer concerns only individual countries, and the answers to our problems have to be found on a world scale.

If we believe that the forces of good prevail over those of evil—and we do believe it—we should not see the year 2000 simply as a challenge to us. The dreams and the images we are already forming of the year 2000 represent the culmination of the twentieth century and usher in the thousand years to come, the age of the progressive development of mankind. Practical measures are already bringing us nearer to it. In an interview with the French newspaper *Le Monde*, on 22 and 23 June 1977, Leonid Brezhnev said that the Soviet Union is preparing a long-term development programme to cover the end of the twentieth century. We look forward to the future with optimism—not a Utopian optimism, but a practical one reflected both in our plans and in our action.

Five-year plans are traditional in the Soviet Union. We have to carry out something like four more before the end of the century. The year 2000 is already quite close. We are moving towards it steadily, and the aims and nature of our progress are reflected in our new Draft Constitution.

Until now, most scientists have not had a very clear idea of the links between the history of man and the history of the earth's biosphere. Since the Soviet scientist V. Vernadsky[1] revealed those links, the study of the biosphere has developed in such a way that today it attracts the interest not only of specialists but also of the public at large.

Vernadsky saw the human race as the 'thinking envelope' of the earth, both a part and the culminating stage of the evolution of the biosphere. He was the first to put forward the idea that the power of man, armed with science and technology, transforms nature and thus becomes comparable to the power of geological forces. The power of man is beginning to determine the evolution of all processes both on earth and in space. Vernadsky went on to say that the despoiling of nature could lead to the exhaustion of earth as a planet for 'living substances', and that man is capable not only of changing the world without harming nature, but also of actually helping nature. In his article on the noosphere (the level of the world on which human activity takes place), Vernadsky wrote: 'The ideals of our democracy are analogous to spontaneous geological processes; the laws of nature correspond to the noosphere.'

The idea of the noosphere implies the necessity for rational organization of the environment.

Because of the great changes brought about by the scientific and technological revolution, we must lose no time

[1] Vladimir Ivanovich Vernadsky (1863–1945), an eminent geochemist and mineralogist, member of the Academy of Sciences of the U.S.S.R.

in solving all these problems. Because we did not foresee the consequences of human activities, and of the despoiling of nature for profit, we have upset the balance between man and the biosphere and mankind now has to face the threat of an ecological explosion.

The ecological crisis is world-wide. The Soviet Union is involved with the rest, but it has considerable resources with which to resist it. The very nature of the Soviet State makes it possible for all our people to 'forge an organic link between the achievements of the scientific and technological revolution and the advantages of the socialist economic system'. The draft of the new Soviet Constitution states:

In the interests of the present and future generations, the necessary steps shall be taken in the U.S.S.R. to protect and make scientifically substantiated, rational use of the land and its minerals, flora and fauna, to preserve the purity of the air and water, ensure the reproduction of natural wealth and man's natural environment.

This method produces unprecedented results. I shall confine myself to one example. It concerns energy sources and the protection of nature. Twenty-three years ago, the Soviet Union built an atomic power station, the first in the world. It informed the Geneva Conference of the experience in the peaceful use of this energy of the future. The President of the Academy of Sciences of the U.S.S.R., Anatoly Petrovich Alexandrov,[2] speaking of the progress of research in this field, said: 'We are nearing the solution of the problem of how to supply mankind with unlimited quantities of electrical energy. The industrial use of the first products of thermonuclear energy could begin towards the end of this century.'

Outside the Soviet Union practical measures against pollution are being taken in many countries, in particular France, Japan, the United States of America and Denmark. But there can be no real solution unless all countries combine their efforts.

I should like to call attention to another kind of pollution —the pollution of the noosphere through the mass media. We should come out against the use of the mass media to propagate racialism and violence, to sow discord between peoples, to incite them against one another, to destroy moral standards—everything aimed at hampering the efforts of people and nations to unite and achieve détente, disarmament, peace and social progress, including an overall solution to ecological problems. We need to carry on an unceasing struggle in this part of the social sphere, the noosphere.

2 Anatoly Petrovich Alexandrov, a physicist and member of the U.S.S.R. State committee for the use of atomic energy.

And art? What will become of that in the year 2000? There are no end of predictions, but I shall not venture to forecast. I should simply like to draw your attention to an interesting trend. Many people think that, by the year 2000, the introduction of new materials will give rise to arts which did not exist before. This may be true. But whatever new materials are invented, art will always come back to man and his sensations, his emotions, his ideas. I do not think art will ever break with the past or set aside the treasures of other ages; rather it will combine bold aspirations with the preservation and development of the traditions of love, of harmony and beauty. I should like to believe that man will save himself and come to feel art as an essential value in life. The men and women of today still try to acquaint themselves with the imperishable treasures of art, both ancient and modern, despite the enormous speeding-up of life which is advocated by the technocrats and deplored by the technophobes, despite the cacaphony of urban existence, despite the gaudy publicity and that confusion of styles and schools as evidenced in exhibitions, which has nothing to do with the multiplicity of art.

Perhaps this is the reason why so many of our contemporaries love the music of Bach and Mozart, the reason why there has been a 'museum explosion', the reason why many young people are so passionately interested in architecture and genuine folk music.

It seems to me that mankind is longing for a renaissance of the cultural and artistic values of past centuries, in order to include them in a flourishing, living culture and make life more beautiful, more humane, more worthy of man. I think the art of the future will be powerful but not coarse, subtle and refined instead of primitive and that it will both recognize and preserve the cultural identity of the different peoples.

In the Soviet Union, side by side with technological and scientific progress, we encourage the development of the arts, both professional and amateur. I would quote, as examples, Palekh miniatures, Viatka toys, *khokhlomas*, Ukrainain embroidery, etc.[3]

More than 20 million people take part in the amateur activities of popular theatres and artistic groups of all kinds; an example of mass cultural development. Not all amateur artists need to become professionals. The main thing is that there should be brought into being in every individual the spirit of creativity which enriches and enobles the whole conception of life.

The intellectual level of the working classes has considerably improved. More than 66 per cent of the workers

3 Palekh miniatures (painted lacquer ware) decorate boxes of differing sizes, often tiny. The traditional wooden toys of Viatka are well known, as are *khokhlomas*, useful or ornamental articles decorated with traditional folk designs.

have completed secondary education, and the young people have all had a general and specialized secondary education. As you know, there is no such thing as unemployment in the Soviet Union. Many workers go on to higher education, though without dropping their professional occupations.

In this way the gap between intellectual work and physical labour is done away with. Work itself calls forth the spirit of initiative and invention, and imparts joy.

As we go forward to the year 2000, our purpose is to enhance the social homogeneity of our society (this is all taken from Article 19 of the Draft Constitution), to erase the distinctions between town and countryside and between labour by brain and by hand; and to develop and draw together all the nations and nationalities of the U.S.S.R.

Giving and sharing

Michiko Inukai

As I reflected upon the theme of this Round Table, two
pictures came up in my mind. One: a gigantic factory
where one of the most sophisticated weapons of our time was
fabricated. This place I visited several years ago in a certain
corner of the earth. The whole building, just like a temple
of Delphi, seemed to be consecrated to the oracle of the
modern deity, Power, and was almost awe-inspiringly
imposing. Hundreds and thousands of people worked there
in somewhat religious serenity, veneration and silence.
Conveyor-belts were everywhere, allowing the numerous
silvery parts of the arms to flow like so many torrents of a
river. There was one part, seemingly an innocent toy of a
child, which, once exploded, could penetrate mortally into
human bodies. There was another, a small spearhead, which
might counteract any missiles of the enemy. Yes, the whole
factory was a temple of dedicated minds and fantastically
developed technology. Billions and billions of dollars were
a daily offering on the altar of this temple.

The other picture that came to my mind was that of a
certain city in a country of heat and humidity, where, under
the burning sun, lying on a pavement, were numerous living
skeletons of men and women, old and young. Some were in
their last agony, some were already unconscious, still others
were expressionless except for their hollow eyes which
looked frantically for some drops of water. Stray dogs were
licking the limbs of some of them. High above the dazzling
blue sky, I saw several vultures flying in a circle, awaiting the
moment to devour their prey. If only these skeletons could
have had, throughout their lifetime, one bowlful of rice and

one glassful of milk every day they would not have lain there to become the prey of the vultures.

Do we survive at all to meet the dawn of the twenty-first century? Or rather, let me put it this way, does humanity have the right to survive to greet a new era? When I think of the power-hungry militarists and certain governments which let themselves be guided by these militarists, pouring millions and millions of money to fabricate sophisticated killing machines to win the arms race, while neglecting the problem of hunger, my answer cannot be but pessimistic, if not negative.

Ever since the creation of the *Dreadnought*, a British destroyer created to meet the challenge of the German navy and considered to be 'all-mighty' at the very beginning of our century, the craze of the arms race has ever been accelerated, and in this craze, the most essential human values have been forgotten. In this craze and fever, the most fundamental elements of true human happiness, namely sharing and mutual respect, fall into oblivion. In this craze, humanity loses its very humanity. (I am not at all a chauvinist but I am extremely proud of the post-war Japanese Constitution in which we, the Japanese, renounce for good any form of participation in the arms race.)[1]

Behind the craze of arms race there is fear, there is hatred —and fear and hatred are negative forces which destroy everything and everyone. Then, indeed then, how can humanity claim to have the right to survival? Where, then, can we find the merit to live long enough to meet the next century?

Power is a blind force. Power is an intoxicating force. Once intoxicated by it, man thinks of nothing else but to seek after more, more, more! In a diary dated somewhere in September 1945, an 8-year-old Japanese boy, then living in the outskirts of a city called Hiroshima, wrote: 'On the 5th August, around 8.15 a.m., the sun exploded, and the world has come to an end....' Yet the atom bomb dropped on this particular morning, accompanied by unthinkable glitter and an ominous mushroom, which swept away in an instant 240,000 lives, is now 500 times smaller than the smallest of the atom bombs possessed by powerful nations. Some talk about 'innocent and clean' hydrogen bombs. Some maintain the logic of the balance of power. Some speak of the nonsense of not being ahead of the times by arms like the hydrogen bomb. Are all these people sane? I wonder.

And a statistic shows that if one-tenth of the cost of armaments (which was in 1975 some $280,000 million) is

1 Article 9 of the Japanese Constitution, which entered into effect on 3 May 1947, spells out the renunciation of war: 'Aspiring sincerely to an international peace based on justice and order, the Japanese people forever renounce war as a sovereign right of the nation and the threat or use of force as means of settling international disputes. In order to accomplish the aim of the preceding paragraph, land, sea and air forces, as well as other war potential, will never be maintained. The right of belligerency of the State will not be recognized.'

spared for a year, then all the living skeletons of starved people, who account for one-third of the total population of the world today, can be decently fed and brought back to normal health. And if another one-tenth is spared, then millions of young minds which do not as yet known the joy of being educated can receive schooling.

Yes, we live in an era in which 'Power' is adored like a goddess. Apart from the power of arms, we can count others immediately; for instance, the power of ever-more colossally growing systems of bureaucracy in whose internal labyrinths individual values and personal dignities are lost; or the power of enormous industries in whose mechanism human morality is but a feeble powerless caricature. There is the power of unthinkably large capital; the power of the mass media and fabricated opinion; the power of ideologies which cannot tolerate or respect the existence of others....

Yes, we do live in an epoch of power-adoration. Adorers are numerous. Yet, fortunately, there is a handful of people who still believe in a human value while rejecting the power-value. Such are the people who gather under the banner of ideas and ideals of the United Nations; such are the obscure people who in an unconspicuous way practice sharing. Here I cannot but recall a letter addressed to me some time ago by a little 10-year-old Japanese boy. He wrote:

Here I enclose some money [equivalent to 5 dollars] which my little brother and I saved by asking our Mother not to give us 4 o'clock cookies for one whole week. Please buy with this money some bread and powdered milk and send them to little boys like me who, unlike me, do not have anything to eat. Mother told us that there were millions of our brothers and sisters in crying need awaiting our help.

Such people not only merit survival, but do create a new order of the world.

Blessed are the poor in spirit. Blessed are they who are kind. Blessed are they who share. Does it sound too Utopian? Too simple? Not at all. On the contrary, such are the only realistic people and realistic ways by which and by whom humanity can save this bent world, to enable it to become more liveable to all men, to remedy all the injustice created by the greed for power.

Yet, I should think that such realistic evangelical ways need some starting-ground or rather, a root. Where can we look for one? Among the metaphysical books? In an elaborated educational system? Here again, my answer is simple enough. A root can be only found in the most basic and vital unit of human communities, namely the family.

In a family that vivid and profound interrelationship of
'you' and 'I' exists: it is lived in a family each moment, while
the modern society of mass communications has long lost a
real intercommunication between persons. 'You', 'I' and
'the others' form a trinitarian communion of mutual respect,
mutual giving and mutual receiving without which human
beings and their society degenerate to a degree of mere
biological existence. In a family there is another sex, another
generation than mine. There are other personalities and
other characters. Each member is different, and precisely
because each is different, a family as a unit is formed. Unity
in diversity. Diversity in unity. In a family, on a family
table, all share what there is to eat. Never once is one
member left out at a mealtime, cast away and condemned
to starve. If one member suffers, all suffer together. If one
rejoices, all rejoice together. Co-operation, collaboration,
giving, sharing, in short love and respect, are the principles
which sustain a family. The 'family' is a prototype of human
society; it is the beginning and the end of it—the only root
of human values.

The family is, also, not an enclosed society but necessarily
open to the socio-economical, politico-cultural outer world,
and to all the problems of others. In family life, a child learns
more and more what it is to be a social being. At the same
time, a home is an oasis where alone, man—especially man
living in an over-industrialized society of hectic rhythm—
can recuperate, can breathe and rest, thus to re-cultivate
himself. A home is the place of birth and rebirth for
'cultured man', in the most basic sense of the word.

And who is the centre, who is the backbone so to speak,
who is the core of the family, of a human home? Woman.

A noted Japanese woman essayist once wrote: 'In the
beginning was the sun.' Why 'the sun'? Because the sun,
just like woman, created life, fosters life, cherishes life, she
gives forth light: in short, she is a positive force, never
negative. A woman, physically as well as psychologically,
is much closer to life than man, together with man she can
accomplish—and is supposed to accomplish—the marvellous
task of letting humanity continue on towards its glorious
destiny.

Woman is very close to love, because of the motherhood
each woman is endowed with by nature. And to me, love is
the only force which can win over the negative force of
power-greed, fear, and hatred, the rejection of others, and
indifference; as love is synonymous with sharing, is synonymous with a capacity to listen to others, is synonymous with
a respect for others, is synonymous with generosity to

2 St Francis of Assisi (1182–1226) is the hero of '*fioretti*', stories of different episodes in his life which were written by three of his closest companions. Many different texts exist of these '*fioretti*' (printed for the first time in 1476), depending upon whether the publisher based himself on one manuscript or another.

acknowledge that even enemies can coexist. The only thing love cannot tolerate is the craze of militarists: the feverish arms race.

Therefore, I would like to conclude with what St Francis of Assisi [2] once said: 'Give us love, O God, so that we may plant love where the forces of evil rule.'

Future $= \dfrac{\Sigma^{\dagger} Pa}{m}$ (past) $+ \dfrac{\Sigma\, Pr}{n}$ (present)[1]

Tchavdar Kuranov

Before broaching the problems with which I intend to deal, namely woman in the year 2000, the expected changes in the character of labour and some problems of leisure, a few words are in order concerning population growth because it is such an important problem. All kinds of calculations and extrapolations are being made as if this process could be directly regulated; but it cannot. It can, however, be regulated indirectly on the basis of social and economic change, as a result of deep social and economic reorganization. If approached out of this context, demography becomes more and more a political tool. It has already been stated that we should adopt a slogan such as: 'There must be more of us in order to survive.' Now, this slogan is a very interesting one if one tries to analyse it. First, it is based on the premise that somebody will survive a nuclear holocaust. Now tell me, you who are specialists, will anybody survive a nuclear holocaust? Second, this slogan may be interpreted (and I give my own interpretation) in the following way: 'We must be more numerous in order to conquer.' In this meaning, population growth may become even equivalent to an arm and this is especially interesting when linked with the foreign policy of a country that is based on the assumption of the inevitability of war. Third, from the slogan 'We must be more numerous in order to survive',[2] there is less than one step to the next probable dictum: 'We must be more numerous to dominate the world.' And this step should not be made. It is the right of all peoples as well as the duty of progressive intellectuals to be very clear on this point, because we want to be and we have to be realistic. Now as

1 The equation used as the title is borrowed from Tchavdar Kuranov, who explains it in these terms: 'The future equals the sum of the whole past divided by m (which is a figure smaller than n) plus the sum of the whole present divided by n (which is a figure bigger than m and smaller than infinity). The meaning is that, according to this equation, the future may be regarded as something equal to much of the past plus some of the present.'

2 T. Kuranov made it clear in a written note that: 'Of course, my negative attitude towards the slogan "Be more in order to survive" is irrespective of the country, the race or the system which might adopt it.'

far as aid is concerned, shall we weigh the aid we give and declare: 'My aid is the best aid in the world'? It is for the developing countries to judge. There is an important neutral indicator: the demand by the less-developed countries for aid from the socialist countries in Eastern Europe and the U.S.S.R. is not declining, it is increasing. This is the realistic indicator. We shall reach the year 2000 in less than twenty-three years, which in terms of planning means in fewer than five five-year plans. If it is true that the future is much of the past and some of the present, let us try to summarize some of the main changes which have occurred in the world in the last twenty-five years. During this period, the scientific and technological revolution began. This was a period of great and rapid economic development. This was a period of social revolution and national liberation which brought to the fore the problem of human equality in a form more acute than during other periods of history. Obviously, the world will continue its development during the next twenty-five years under the impact of these main trends, and this impact may have a cumulative effect in the solution of some important problems until the year 2000: (a) a change in the status of women in human society, as a part of the social revolution; (b) changes in the character of labour as a result of the scientific and technological revolution; (c) a new concept of leisure resulting from economic development. But all this is on the assumption that there will be peace, peaceful co-existence and détente. Some are afraid of this, and I really do not know why. We must analyse the possible alternatives. What are they? Cold war? It has already been tried. Did it have important results? Perhaps war plain and simple? If these are the alternatives I know that the majority will be and are in favour of détente. I see nothing dangerous in this. Now, what shall we choose? Not to exist or to coexist? Of course, some may choose the first possibility, but I choose the latter, and this time this freedom of choice is not democratic choice, it is either a humanitarian solution excluding the possibility of nuclear holocaust or a non-humanitarian solution to the problems of the future.

The industrial revolution of the nineteenth century changed the status of only a portion of women and gave birth to the image of the woman factory worker. The scientific and technological revolution of the mid-1950s is constantly changing the status of all women, giving birth to the image of the working woman in general. This change in status from housewife to working woman, which is of such a decisive character, causes other changes. Participation in the labour process requires participation in public and political life. But the two new roles of women as workers outside the household and participants in public life cannot liberate them from their role as wives and mothers which consequently increases their burden. How will this contradiction be solved over the next twenty-five years, as more women both in the developed and developing countries enter the labour market and political life? The next twenty-five years should constitute a period in which this new division of labour between man and woman outside the household, when both of them work, is reflected by a new division of labour inside the household, where labour will cease to be the dubious privilege of women. Such changes in the roles of women mean that during the next twenty-five years, they will adopt a new profile neither based on the three Ks *Küche, Kinder, Kirche*, the ideal of the *petit bourgeois*, nor on the model of the playgirl, the sex bomb, nor again on the model of the highly cultivated and cultured woman who remains all her life a consumer of commodities and ideas. It will be a combination of all the three roles of women as workers, as politically active social beings and as mothers. But participation of women in the production process does not mean that they should be treated as child-bearing machines. Society must create conditions in which the combination of these three roles can be attained in such a way as to ensure the development of woman's personality, her individual qualities as a human being. Societies which are the first to realize these necessities and create adequate conditions for them will probably have a great advantage. And I think that there are sound reasons for us to expect that by the year 2000, the model of woman based on the triple principle of work outside the home, social political activity and motherhood, will become the prevailing rule in human society.

Coming to some problems of labour, there exist qualitative differences between societies representing different social and economic systems. It would be Utopian to expect, in the time remaining until the year 2000, changes that would abolish the compulsory character of labour, but it is realistic to expect some important changes in this field. One aspect of the problem is the fact that in many countries of the world, people are suffering, not because of the compulsion to work but precisely because they cannot become the subject and the object of such compulsion, because they remain for long periods outsiders to the labour process. Concealed agrarian unemployment in the less-developed countries is a sinister illustration of this situation, and without the involvement of millions of people in the labour process, on a more or less permanent and regular basis, the rate of growth in the less-developed countries will not be able to attain goals which alone can stop the widening of the gap between them and the developed countries. According to the Leontief report, issued this year, 6 per cent annual per capita rate of growth for the developing countries, coupled with a 3.5 per cent growth rate in the developed nations, is the only possible way to reduce by half the difference in income between them. And this goal cannot be met if the employment in the less-developed countries remains as low as it is now. Such changes, however, would not occur if both technological change and deep social reforms—the latter being of decisive importance—do not take place. And the same Leontief report stresses that to ensure accelerated development, two general conditions are necessary: first, far-reaching internal changes of a social, political and institutional character in the developing countries; and second, significant changes in the world economic order. One of the most important features of such changes should be the involvement of broad masses of people in the labour process assuring extensive economic growth with high rates. If this does not occur at least to a large extent before the year 2000, it will mean backwardness and starvation in the less-developed countries. This problem has another aspect in the developed countries. Experience has shown that for some of the developed countries—especially for some of the most developed—unemployment caused by the business cycle remains one of the most acute problems. Under the existing socio-economic structure in these countries, the development of technology has brought no solution. Certain changes in the socio-economic structure as well as in production relations would be expected to occur, so as to open new possibilities for the development of technology. It is more or less accepted that technological development is leading toward automation. Without over-estimating automation, but assuming that it will continue to develop at a rapid rate, we may expect an even higher rate of unemployment. But it is becoming more and more difficult for society to accept this responsibility. World opinion is becoming increasingly aware that the unemployed are not a reserve army, but human beings. As this idea grips the masses, it is turning into a material force that cannot be counterbalanced by oppression and violence. One solution might be the constant support of the unemployed, at the expense of society, which constitutes however discrimination against the employed. Another solution might be found in shortening the working week, but this pertains mainly to those in material production. Yet another solution might be to divide all the necessary time for material production among the total labour force whether in material production or not. And such a solution which is not impossible under automated conditions and conditions of socio-economic change, would probably lead to a decisive decrease in the compulsory character of labour.

Leisure is usually considered in contrast to labour: the less you work, the more leisure you have. This is quite so when labour occupies 50–80 per cent or even more of man's active day (not counting the eight hours reserved for biological needs). But if automation should succeed in decreasing labour time, by half or even more (Tomaso Campanelle mentioned four hours, August Bebel three, while Robert Owen spoke of two),[3] the attitude towards leisure will change. Its quantitative increase would give rise to new non-compulsory activities or the transformation of labour into creative activities. Creating itself would have relatively increasing significance but for this to be achieved, technology and automation would have to be developed to such an extent as to enable compulsory labour to be decreased considerably. Consequently the pseudo-logical maxim—'The less you work, the more leisure you have'—would be replaced by a logical one—'The more you work, the more leisure you have.' This is not abstract reasoning. Even now in some of the most developed countries, a human being devotes about 120,000–140,000 labour hours during his lifetime to material production, while in a less-developed country, such as ours, this figure amounts to only about 80,000 labour hours. It is much less in the developing countries. Usually in the most developed countries, the possibilities for leisure, especially active leisure, are greater. In a less-developed country, people work less and rest less. The decrease of compulsory labour will give rise to new possibilities for the increase of non-compulsory labour, creating an important reserve for the increase of overall labour inputs. But the qualitatively important aspect for creative activities, creation, would come with the increased possibilities resulting from the growing share of non-compulsory labour. For this reason, I think that the role of Unesco is going to grow in importance, because Unesco is the international body most closely connected with creativeness, with the creative role of man. This will not all happen by the year 2000 or even immediately after, but the possibilities of technological and socio-economic development are such now that all of what I have said here does not seem to me to be Utopian, provided human society realizes

3 In the Utopian universe of Campanella (*Civitas Solis*), the division of labour and community living reduce the amount of work to be done by women (who are nevertheless subject to a specific obligation, namely that of selective reproduction, the authority deciding by which man a woman should have children, though she is otherwise free to use her body as she wills).

Bebel's estimate in his work *Die Frau und der Sozialismus* (Women and Socialism) (1879), where he quotes the evaluation of Robert Owen (cf. *A New View of Society* and *The New Moral World*). In a science-fiction novel, *Les Hommes Frénétiques* (1924), Ernest Pérochon, a French teacher and writer of socialist tendencies, appears to have reached the limit when describing, in a highly technological society, a workers' demonstration amidst shouts of 'A one-hour day or death!'

the importance of social change, provided also that human society does not destroy itself.

Up until now, the main source of knowledge of mankind has been the past: mankind has been able to see its present mainly through the prism of the past. It is, however, extremely necessary for mankind to be able to see its present through the prism of the future.

Catching
our second wind

M. L. Mehrotra

The universal human desire is for peace, happiness, harmony and eternal ecstasy. Everyone tries to work towards these objectives whether it be in his home, in the community, in national or international relations. But in spite of the best efforts harmony and eternal ecstasy seem to elude us.

Now in going into the ancient writings of Rig-Vedas, which give a description of knowledge in the year 2300 B.C., the sources and outline of the production and uses of all types of energy, including atomic energy, are clearly indicated. Due to the feuds amongst two major prevailing groups of people, the technical processes and knowledge were destroyed by Janamejaya. [1]

The sources of energy are also described in the fourth chapter of that great epic, the *Gita*. The processes of production, control and use of energy were not passed on from the few sages to others for the simple reason that man had started using technology both against his brother and against nature. We are hopeful that history will not repeat itself. At the present time, nuclear arms are designed for use against man, and it is up to world opinion to put an end to the stock piles of weapons.

The movement of the universe, based on certain scientific and technological principles, is in the hands of God, by whom the sun was entrusted with the production and distribution of energy, for the entire energy of this universe is located in the sun.

Instead of utilizing this tremendous source of fresh energy we have been ceaselessly running after and exploiting fossil energy and creating ecological or environmental

1 According to tradition, it was in the presence of King Janamejaya that the *Mahabharata* was recited for the first time. This Sanskrit epic poem is probably the longest in world literature (200,000 lines). It is attributed to Vyasa the Wise and is thought to date from the beginning of the second millennium B.C. King Janamejaya was the grandson of one of the *Mahabharata* heroes, the warrior Arjuna. The Bagavad Gita, an episode of the *Mahabharata*, includes religious and philosophical concepts in addition to traditional history and legend.

problems while gradually destroying the stability of the planet.

Being a lung specialist, I would like to point out that the lung membranes are the most extensible of all body tissues that intervene directly between man and his environment.

The lung surface membrane is as large as a tennis court and is exposed daily to a volume of air and contaminants that would fill a swimming pool. The extent to which the infectious agents, chemical toxics, fine dust and minerals breach the defenses of the lungs, determines the development of respiratory disease—tuberculosis, bronchitis, silicosis, smoker's bronchitis, emphysema and asthma—that make life unbearable. The polluting agents of the environment not only reduce the capabilities of the lungs, but also alter the development of immunity and effectiveness of the lung's defences.

On an average nearly 50 per cent of energy is utilized by industry, 25 per cent for transportation and another 25 per cent for domestic consumption. In the developed countries the per capita annual energy consumption in terms of coal is approximately 6,000 kilograms, and the per capita annual income about $3,000. In contrast to this, we have a ratio of 200 kilograms and $100 in the developing countries.

I believe that excessive disparity in income, in energy exploitation and consumption is not conducive to human happiness throughout the world. The economics of developing countries cannot increase conventional energy production twenty-five to thirty times within the next twenty-five years, and that is what they require. But they should not pattern their life-style on that of industrialized countries.

People have lived for thousands of years in small self-educated communes and villages—of which we in India have more than half a million—which will have a total projected population in the year 2000 of 1,100 million people. Power plants and transmission networks necessary for domestic fuel, lighting, agriculture and small and medium industries are beyond the reach of the present economy and technology. Yet, if they are not provided, there will continue to be an increasing trend towards urbanization, bringing in its wake innumerable problems of health, housing, transportation and communications.

Therefore something has to be done. We have to develop solar power technology with energy collectors to convert heat to electricity, so that village and inaccessible communities do not have to depend on conventional power plants and transmission lines. Each village could then have its own solar power plant and be independent of others in establishing power plants and transmission networks and in maintaining them.

The environmental hazards of coal and nuclear power-plants would be eliminated with solar energy and existing life-styles in rural areas would not undergo such drastic change.

The bio-gas plants, of which more than 10,000 have already been installed in certain villages, have proved success-ful. They are clean and also prevent environmental degra-dation by burning animal dung and wood obtained after felling trees. However, there are problems in obtaining mass supplies of simple equipment, problems arising from co-operative functioning between households and training users (people are still not willing to have the power plants in the villages). So that is a big problem. But they function very satisfactorily.

Hydrogen power could be another alternative to solar energy as it is non-polluting. Liquid hydrogen fuel can be transported in pipelines and can be produced by hydrolysis wherever there is plentiful water. But again the problem is that large on-shore platforms and power are required to produce the reaction and people would be dependent on this centralized production and subsequent distribution.

Nuclear energy, both fission (conventional and fast-breeder reactors) and future fusion reactors, is the current craze, with fusion reactors possible by the turn of the century. But the main problem is long gestation and stockpiling of nuclear arms which destroy man and nature and may lead to the same situation as happened 5,300 years ago.

As regards transportation, unless stored energy is used, the emphasis will have to be on public rather than private transportation, because the cost of transporting the same number of people is fifty to a hundred times less and private transportation is a hundred times more polluting, virtually destroying the lungs and making them prone to disease.

As regards urban planning, that also has to undergo a drastic change. With the development of solar power plants, houses will be of one or two storeys with de-emphasis on high-rise buildings. Cities will have to be small, the maximum population being limited to half a million people spread out in a radius of five kilometres, twenty or thirty kilometres apart so that the environment is not disturbed or polluted.

Use of energy is desirable to enjoy nature and to achieve peace of mind and happiness, but the fundamental question is: how much and what type of energy is needed so that the necessary objectives can be adhered to? Obviously very little energy is needed to achieve human happiness, but people must accept the philosophy of Mahatma Gandhi:[2] minimum needs and hence minimum heavy industrialization, creation of small autonomous self-reliants units, tolerance and respect for all life, human, and plant, and thus the least disturbance possible of nature and the environment.

How can the problems of the year 2000 be met? We feel by responding collectively to the challenges of the future, by accepting responsibility for reduction of economic disparities, by keeping needs to a minimum, by conserving energy, by utilizing the local available energy resources, developing self-reliance and energy self-sufficiency, by establishing national energy institutes and sharing technology. In countries like ours, by the establishment of independent rural energy centres in every village and what is most important, by educating the masses throughout the world to resist the generation of energy from sources which pollute the environment for human, animal and plant life. And again, by creating a world-wide awareness about environmental pollution and its effects on all living objects in the area.

These pressing problems must be fully understood and the challenge met. To give you an example, you remember that as a result of a mandate from WHO, in a period of three years smallpox, which had been out of control for more than a hundred years, was brought under control. Many of the challenges I have mentioned can only be met by means of a global concept and mandate. Unesco is the proper body to initiate appropriate action on almost all the points just mentioned.

2 It may be mentioned that the mahatma, for whom no subject was negligible, wrote a 'guide to health' which can profitably be re-read in the light of 'soft technology' research likely to assist in restoring man's physical and moral balance as well as that of society and the environment.

The ultimate selection

Nancy Reeves

Students of the human condition, I should like to begin with a quotation from one of the *Four Quartets*[1] by T. S. Eliot. He said:

> ... Had they deceived us
> Or deceived themselves, the quiet-voiced elders,
> Bequeathing us merely a receipt for deceit?
> The serenity only a deliberate hebetude,
> The wisdom only the knowledge of dead secrets
> Useless in the darkness into which they peered
> Or from which they turned their eyes. There is
>   it seems to us,
> At best, only a limited value
> In the knowledge derived from experience.
> The knowledge imposes a pattern, and falsifies,
> For the pattern is new in every moment
> And every moment is a new and shocking
> Valuation of all we have been....

That's my first text. My second text is taken from Melville's *Moby Dick*[2] where Captain Ahab simply says: 'All my means are sane, my motive and my object mad.' The reflections I wish to share with you resulted from a conference on the future of the West which was composed principally of political leaders and political scientists. I was struck by the endless weaving and reweaving of a web of ideas derived from the past. In contrast, there was a talk by an astronomer. He showed, with slides, how the earth appeared from space, a small, blue, vulnerable planet with a thin layer of atmosphere and a thin crust of matter, to support life. Then he

1 Quotation from *East Coker* (1940), one of the *Four Quartets*, the other three being *Burnt Norton* (1941), *The Dry Salvages* (1941) and *Little Gidding* (1942).

2 *Moby Dick*, the most famous of Herman Melville's works, was published in 1851.

offered what he termed the cosmic calendar, compressing the 15,000-million-year existence of our universe into a single twelve-month period. I think it was his way of deprovincializing the present for these political scientists. 'In the time span of one year', he said, 'in that twelve-month time span, the earth does not condense out of interstellar matter until early September: dinosaurs emerge on Christmas Eve; flowers arise on the 28 December; and men and women originate at 10.30 p.m. on New Year's Eve. All of recorded history occupies the last ten seconds of 31 December; and the time from the waning of the Middle Ages to the present occupies little more than one second.' But because he had arranged it that way, the first cosmic year has just ended. 'And despite the insignificance of the instant we have so far occupied in cosmic time, it is clear that what happens in and near the earth at the beginning of this, the second cosmic year, will depend very much on the scientific wisdom and distinctly human sensitivity of mankind.' Then came a question period and I was struck by the irrelevance of the questions, by the way the political scientists and the political leaders responded to the astronomer's frame of reference. And I asked myself, were they avoiding the message or did they fail to comprehend it? And that is how I started my intellectual journey.

For at the simplest level, at the intrinsic level, I was startled by the style of reasoning of the political scientists and of the political leaders. First, in terms simply of their definition of the situation; then in terms of the date bearing on the situation and finally on the options for the future which flowed from these assumptions. In my judgement, every test of rigour in conceptual thought was violated.

First the Baconian fallacies were violated and because they are not taught anymore, maybe I should list them: the fallacy of *secundum quid*, or founding a sweeping generalization on the basis of a few specifics (I have heard such reasoning many times at the United Nations); the fallacy of *ignoratio elenchi*, which is divided into *ad hominem*, or attacking the character of a person to win a point, *ad populum*, appealing to the crowd, and *ad baculum*, appealing to fear; the fallacy of *ad vericundiam*, especially significant in this context, because it means appealing to revered authority, and certainly they were all revered authorities there; the fallacy *petitio principii*, or begging the question, which also embraces *circulus in probando*, or the conclusion is contained in the premises; and finally the fallacy *post hoc ergo propter hoc*, after this, therefore because of this—unforgettably illustrated by Chantecler in Rostand's play, [3] who noticed that after he crowed, the sun rose, and therefore concluded that it was because he crowed that the sun had risen.

They also cherished the idols, the idols of the cave, the idols of the tribe, the idols of the market-place, and most particularly the idols of the theatre which, Bacon said, in his *Novum Organum*, [4] illustrate all received systems as 'so many stage plays representing worlds of their own creation after an unreal and scenic fashion'. There was, in addition, another type of reasoning that I was interested to discover coming up over and over again in the discussion, the pattern of thinking in polarities, dichotomies and binary categories, East against West, capitalism against communism, democracy against tyranny. It illustrated the reflective distance between ideas derived from Aristotle and those rooted in Galilean and post-Galilean physics. For in physics since Galileo, not only is nothing *a priori* or unimportant or trivial, but dichotomous classifications have been replaced by concepts of continuous gradation. Phenomena can be understood only if they are seen in continuous variation, with transition stages always present. Developments of quantum physics, for example, have carried this still further, the concepts of the necessity of including time in the description of phenoma, of the possible importance of the seemingly trivial, and of description in terms not of polarities, not of dualities, but of continuous gradation. In this sense, reality in this newer scientific perspective is phrased in terms of interaction rather than separation, continuities rather than polarities, multiple possibilities rather than dualities. I think one rarely encounters this in political discussions.

On the other hand, the idea of compromise in a political discussion is considered to be equivocation. In that sense, compromise is a pejorative term in politics and a reasonable term in bargaining about money. If you bargain about money, even at the legislative level, you strike a figure in between the two extremes, that is considered practical. If you do it in terms of concepts, it is considered surrender. I think that good reasoning requires parallel methods of mediating conflicting positions, or at least of exploring the distance, the actual distance between them.

Such procedures are imperative not only in relation to conflict resolution, but in relation to reality, because abstract categories applied to concrete conditions deform truth and those who employ them are unaware of change and of the impact of the pace of change. Consider centralized production with its bureaucratic gears. It has affected the structure of systems irrespective of ideology. The bureau-

3   The hymn to the sun in Chantecler (1910), with its famous refrain: '*O soleil, Toi sans qui les choses ne seraient que ce qu'elles sont*' (Oh sun, thou without whom things would be but what they are).

4   *Novum Organum or New Method for the Interpretation of Nature* (1620).

cracy follows on the process. Similarly, global technology, with its planetary impact, has vanquished isolated habitats irrespective of geography. Yet, at the conference, political figures at the pinnacles of power and their professional theorists were locked into a static view of the species which was time-bound and space-bound. Their discourse was predictable not predictive and even in dispute became a speculative elaboration of a few elementary assumptions.

I think that the discussion was specious, I think the reasoning was specious, but it was also constrained by a very narrow philosophical foundation. Long ago, White-head [5] said: when questioning the ideas of an epoch, do not focus on those positions that are explicitly defended. Rather, he said, 'There will be some fundamental assumptions which adherents of all the various systems . . . unconsciously presuppose. Such assumptions appear so obvious that people do not know what they are assuming because no other way of putting things has ever occurred to them.' I began to wonder what were the basic assumptions that the various political figures and their theorists at this conference had, so that no other way of putting things had ever occurred to them. And I came up with a strange one, perhaps, I think there was an assumption of special creation, not so much in the religious sense as in the charmed sense: that a man was not, that the species was not subject to the laws of science and the laws of change. I am sure that all of the participants had encountered the Darwinian heresy. I am sure that they had been exposed to evolutionary principles in their school-days, if not later, but they did not see life as 'multitudinous and emergent in the stream of time' and this foreshortened possibility. And it also overlooked the process and the mode of selection for survival in the evolution of man.

Because we sometimes forget that *homo sapiens* is a culture-bearing animal, that it is the nature of *homo sapiens* to be culture-bearing. This quality is not something pasted on top of the animal. Survival was determined by that particular selection, and man in nature is not distinguishable from man in culture. It is the nature of man to be cultural. It follows that the concept of culture is as necessary as the concept of evolution to an understanding of the distinctively human aspects of human biology.

Nature lives in motion. But I think what is frequently overlooked is that culture also lives in motion, and culture is the human being's second nature. Offhand one would say that the rise and fall of civilizations is apparent to everyone, at the institutional surface of human history. But I think the dynamics of evolutionary change, in the sense of reality

5   Alfred North Whitehead (1861–1947), the English philosopher and mathematician, was one of the founders of mathematical logic. *Modes of Thought* (1938) is one of his most considerable works.

transformation, is not so easily perceived. And I say this because of the simple equivalences that are offered from one period to another, the cyclic idea of history that one can lift the notion of democracy in a city-State and apply it to a huge nation—this is, I think, a deformation of reality. And yet, at the conference, it was constantly done, as people sought guides from the past for our unprecedented social dilemma. Long ago, Wallace[6] perceived that man had transferred to his machines and tools many of the alterations of parts that in animals take place through the evolution of the body. It is a different kind of mutation, technological mutation, evolving from cultural ideas which change ecological possibilities. We have the prostheses of machines, the adaptations of ecosystems. But the signal novelty is that each advance in coping makes nature less determinative. As the culture progresses, nature becomes less determinative, culture becomes more determinative. We are less prisoners of nature; we are more prisoners of the culture we invent. Analogy, therefore, from the determinative precedents of one period to another, cannot really be made. It is a misapplication, because by the time you move in time, you have another determinative culture. As technology becomes more sophisticated, the patterns of imperative, the spheres of action, are continually transformed, until we reach the stage of the current crisis where it becomes possible for the very existence of the species to be determined by our own decisions. That is why I called this paper 'The Ultimate Selection'. As Eiseley[7] says:

We are now in a position to see the wonder and terror of the human predicament: man is totally dependent on society. Creature of dream, he has created an invisible world of ideas, beliefs, habits and customs which buttress him about and replace for him the precise instincts of the lower creatures. In this invisible universe he takes refuge, but just as instinct may fail an animal under some shift of environmental conditions, so man's cultural beliefs may prove inadequate to a new situation.

No doubt that is what we are here about.

I think that I should like to move at this point to the idea that it has always been that way, we have always faced crises, we have always faced catastrophes. That may be true. But we were not globally a single ecosystem. If there was a catastrophe in a single habitat, there might be destruction of that group, but never before in the history of the species has a global catastrophe implied extinction of the species on the habitat we call earth. Yes we know this. At one level, of course, it has been said and we know it. It was even the

6 The English naturalist Alfred Wallace (1823–1916).

7 L. C. Eiseley, American anthropologist and historian.

theme of the conference I am describing, 'The Future of the West', and yet the conviction that one could have a future of the West without a future of the globe was inherent, even in the title. On 20 June the *Los Angeles Times* reported that Dean Rusk, one of the conference participants and former Secretary of State in our country, had referred to energy problems as 'a new cause of war coming down the road'. Clearly to him conflict resolution is to be resolved by conflict. He went on to say 'long before that happens [the end of energy] nations of the world are going to be at each other's throats' for energy supplies. It is a troubling thought that conflict of position should be perceived by decision-makers as leading inexorably to a single form of resolution. And I have begun to think it is a result not simply of a kind of contemporary tribalism, which seems to be increasing all the time, or even of a kind of atomism, but of an inability to look below the surface of cherished ideas, and I believe it comes from a profound ignorance of the meaning of science in society.

I do not mean here exactly knowing the formula for H_2O, although most of the decision-makers probably do not know that either, but the methodology of science as a way of validating reality, of testing assumptions, of making hypotheses and coming to conclusions. I think the scientific illiteracy of statesmen in a world civilization powered by sciences in the philosophical as well as the technological sense, is a horrendous truth. I remember how President Nixon dismissed his scientific advisers when they told him something he did not wish to hear. It is like the divine right of kings: off with his head when someone incurred royal displeasure. Messenger was identified with message. Nor can the prejudices and impurities incorporated in the universe of options that results from this kind of attitude be shifted without shifting the basic frame of reference. It is imperative to get back to what Whitehead has called 'the irreducible and stubborn facts'. And politicians do not deal with irreducible and stubborn facts.

Carl Sagan, who was the astronomer I mentioned earlier, asked at one point: cannot politics ever be characterized as wrong? And of course the answer is, 'no'. Politics do not seek truth or error, right or wrong; politics seek to win or lose. It is an entirely different frame of reference, and we are at a point where the win and lose frame of reference of the people who are making decisions can no longer be applied without peril to the conditions we have inherited. When Sagan finished, he proposed that we start having experiments on ideological matters, on political matters, using the kinds of technique that are well-known in science, so that we can test some of these dogmas that are treated like religious truths, more or less, or like myths or taboos. Let us have some kind of validated experiment, let us test within a framework of controlled variables, let us find out what our options are. I liked that idea and I telephoned him before I came and asked: do you have one specific experiment I could offer at Unesco (because he had said we need about fifty to test inherited ideas that are always asserted and never validated)? And he answered: no, he had already gone out of his field in offering the idea, He would not design an experiment, but Dr Sagan did suggest that we could, at a conference like this, begin by convening a conference to design the first experiment. Such a conference, he said, should include ten to fifteen specialists, but not culture-bound specialists. He specially warned about that. People at the cutting edge of change, people who are not like T. S. Eliot's elders, so locked into the past that they could not move into a new frame of reference. He also suggested that such a sociological experiment might find volunteers among the youth to carry it out. Usually a Round Table ends with the exchange of ideas, sometimes, if we are lucky, there is a synthesis, a building of brick on brick. I should like to propose that we initiate such a project as part of our work.

Sagan also described the MacLean model of the triune brain.[8] I will not go into that in detail because it may be tiring for you, but the triune brain concept provides a kind of evolution. When we develop a new mechanical appliance, when we get tired of some technological machine and invent a new one, that is change. In evolution, however, the process is different, the old forms are retained and new forms are laid over them and the triune brain is thus composed of the reptilian brain, which is called the R-complex, surrounded by the limbic brain which we got from the giant sloths, and finally by the neocortex. And Dr Sagan suggested that the salvation of mankind might depend on our relinquishment of the R-complex or the reptilian brain which he thinks most political decision-makers use, and begin to use the part of the brain that we have been mainly selected for, the part that will determine our survival, the neocortex. So I would like to combine these two ideas: first the utilization of the neocortex, and second, that we begin to think of the scientific method as a way of approaching truth, and that we initiate concrete experiments to test out some of our more cherished ideas. Because long ago, Kirkegaard observed: 'He who fights the future has a

8   In connection with the 'triune brain', a recent article (in *Le Monde* (Paris) on 8 September 1977) by Dr François Jacob, who received the Nobel prize in physiology and medicine in 1975, states: 'The old controlling structure in lower mammals has, so to speak, been put on the emotional shelf. In humans, it has become what the neuro-biologist MacLean calls "the visceral brain". The development of the human being is characterized by extreme slowness and late maturity. It is perhaps for that reason that the old structures have retained close connections with the primal autonomous centres, that they continue co-ordinating such basic activities as food-seeking, the search for a sexual partner or the reaction to an enemy. The formation of the dominant neocortex, coupled with the continuation of a nervous and hormonal system which is not only ancient but also partially autonomous—all this leaves the impression of a haphazard evolutionary process. It is almost as if someone installed a jet engine on a horse-drawn cart. It is not surprising there are accidents.'

dangerous enemy. The future is not, it borrows its strength from the man himself and when it has tricked him out of this, then it appears outside of him as the enemy he must meet.' The ultimate selection of *homo sapiens* has been the capacity of his brain, particularly of the neocortex. With a modicum of insight, with a maximum of daring, we can prevent the future from becoming an enemy; we can prevent the planet from becoming the ultimate selection, in the holocaust sense, by using the ultimate selection of the brain, in the evolutionary one.

Mobilizing the resources of man's whole being

Prem Kirpal

Never before the emergence of our own contemporary age was it possible to consider consciously, systematically and synthetically the challenge to man and his larger society from a global, even cosmic point of view. Contemporary man has to seek his salvation along with the salvation of his society, and apart from his local and national homes, his global habitat is now a reality. Both his scope of action and responsibility of choice have taken a universal dimension of possibilities and consequences. In the past thoughtful persons living beyond the prison of the passing moment and seeking some unattainable vision have speculated over the future of their own life spans and the mystery beyond life and death; but never before have they probed into the living problems of all humanity or even their own civilization or culture in order to find solutions and plan for appropriate action.

This has been achieved by the growing awareness of man about his own personal nature, about his larger society and culture and about the whole of humanity. We partake of many diversities in an overall unity of similar concerns and a common bondage. The interdependence of nations and the solidarity of mankind are sensed far more keenly and seen in so many more tangibles by contemporary man than by his forebears of the past.

In addition to this shrinkage of space in the mind of man and his daily concerns, contemporary man has established a new relationship with time. Different cultures have viewed the phenomenon of time in diverse ways, but all men and women of our time, sharing the universal advance of science and technology and the explosion of knowledge, can confidently feel that man is now, more than ever before, a maker of his own destiny, a conscious and masterful agent in the process of evolution. The fulfilment of this destiny calls for new capacities, responsibilities and duties, which are not beyond his grasp and performance now.

We must now move towards a greater synthesis of life by a wise and orderly convergence of its many parts and seek the wholeness of man in the integration of his inner being and his outer environment. The union of science and spiruality poses a challenge which is both enormous and exciting. The dominance of the economic man which still persists in the habits and institutions of our industrial, money-making and power-grabbing past can now give way to the shaping of a more integrated man, preferring the richness and wholeness of the quality of life to the mindless production and consumption of material goods in a debasing spirit of acquisition and greed, leading always to tension and conflict.

The challenging implications of these contemporary developments, concerning deeply the inner man and his outer environment of people in his time and space, call urgently for accurate knowledge and deep wisdom in order to act together for the creation of a new man and a new world order.

This is how I see the real and living context of our tasks, which cannot be a mere exercise of the mind in the subtleties of thought, but should find a clear and abiding focus of some superhuman action and purposeful creation.

Many challenges face us and more can emerge as we move towards the year 2000 which is surely a part of our own time even if some of us will not be alive in temporal existence to partake of its climax and adventure. To my mind three great challenges loom large and continually gather force; for me the third of these, the making of the inner man in his moral and spiritual entity, is the most crucial problem.

The three great challenges confronting man and his societies can be briefly stated as follows.

Man's physical survival. This is perilously endangered by a trinity of evil forces that are not unrelated. Three forces are: (a) the terrible consequences of the armaments race and man's mad and increasing investment in the power house of death and destruction—which draws an enormous part of his intellect and wealth; (b) the dangers of unbridled consumerism which lead to waste and pillage of nature and decadence of man's moral and spiritual nature; (c) the persistence of poverty and sheer starvation among large sections of humanity when some optimum well-being is clearly within the reach of all if we can only act wisely in a spirit of sharing together and mutual co-operation.

Man's moral integrity. Here too the challenge to man's moral integrity assumes three important forms: (a) care for human dignity by battling against misery and wretchedness and recognizing the innate worth of all living beings; (b) promotion and defending freedom, which is the birthright of all and also an essential condition of any worthwhile civilization and cultures; (c) attaining a larger measure of equality and social justice within each society and among all societies of both the so-called developed and developing nations.

Man as a spiritual entity. The overriding factor in the making of civilization is always the spirit of man, which is now unfortunately depressed and threatened by his technology and institutional network of power and vested interest. More than anything else we need now to assert the primacy of man's immortal spirit and his precious spiritual entity by exploring and developing the inner man which is the source of creativity and transcendence. For me the foremost challenge of the year 2000 is the discovery and affirmation of man's spirituality and bringing it into full play in the marvellous play of life and for the attainment of some new leap forward in creation and transcendence. Only such an affirmation and transcendence can solve the numerous problems that bedevil us in the process of temporal life, and threaten man's essential moral nature and even his physical survival.

How can we go about meeting this supreme challenge of affirming and generating man's spirituality for a greater quality of life, a new civilization of order and beauty and the best refinements and creative sparks of culture?

At this point I wish to present a statement on *Toward Creativity and Transcendence in Search of the Inner Man* which I wrote for myself in a dark moment of the integrity and freedom of my national society. I present this here because it is relevant to the larger purpose of the Round Table and in particular to my viewpoint of the overriding challenge of the year 2000:

When things go wrong in the normal working of human affairs and the business of day-to-day living becomes sour and bleak to the taste and the eye, it is good to think of the larger dimensions of existence that are always with us but tend to fall into oblivion in the passion and frenzy of living and in the rush of the 'get and grab' tempo of daily life, inspired by the rather low pursuits of power and acquisition.

Beyond the dimension of the present moment of temporal existence filled by the needs of the body and its earthy drives of flesh and lucre, there are always two other dimensions, the cosmic and the elemental, to which we belong, deeply and irrevocably, and in a sense more intense and relevant than the seeming immersion in the temporal. To ignore and forget these realities of our external home in the cosmos and our origins in the elements of nature and heredity is to invite disaster to the integrity and wholeness of the human person. The lure of temporal existence, dominated by the pursuit of power and the might of technology, and obsessed with the needs and desires of life experienced in moments and fragments, deludes us into such a condition.

Let us think of the larger dimensions of the cosmos and of the elements of our being beyond the plight of the temporal in the present moment.

The cosmic dimension of my life relates me to the vast totality of awareness received through the mind and the senses from all the known wonders of the sciences, the arts and the humanities, and the warmth of sheer living and human relationships experienced in an ever-growing sensitivity of the spirit. It also includes the consciousness of the ultimate mystery, which may remain distant and unfathomed, but can never disappear or become insignificant. In fact, the more we know and experience the greater is the consciousness of the mysterious, and the best perspective of life often emerges from the living reality of the mysterious, felt and experienced vividly alongside the luminosity of knowledge and the intensity of sensual awareness. The cosmic dimension, therefore, comprehends both reason and faith, science and poetry. My cosmos is truly a world of great wonder and greater mystery in which I can sense the infinitely larger whole of which I am a tiny fragment and thus feel in this keen sense of belonging what one may call the sanctity and unity of life. The cosmic dimension brings experience of timelessness in love, worship and beauty. It calls for several ways and moods for its revelation, the ways of reason and faith, the moods of active strife and patient waiting, depending upon one's condition, choice and temperament. Each one develops his own way and style of transcendence in the pursuit of the same urge for reaching beyond the self and its present predicament to higher dimensions of awareness and vision.

For me the daily offering of solitude and meditation is always an attempt at merging into the cosmic; the passing events assume their true proportion and meaning only in the awareness of the cosmic, which relates the trivial and the transitory to its inner core of meaning and timelessness; and the day's brief passage flows into the endless stream of history by the magic touch of the cosmic which is always with us but is seldom recognized and employed in the business of daily living. Now it is time to turn to the cosmic dimensions of life and brood over its mystery in wonder, enjoy the marvel of its contemplation, and probe deep into its essence.

The elemental dimension is also a reality to be reckoned with, an essential part of existence. While the cosmic partakes largely of the world of the mind and the spirit, the elemental dimension is comprised of the seed and sap of life and the essence of the life-force. I mentioned above that the main components of the elemental are nature and heredity. Nature is the larger environment of our earthly habitat from which we derive our biological origins and our sustenance through life. Heredity conditions within certain limits our individual make-up and offers participation in the life of the past—the past of our tribes and societies, and, indeed, of the entire human species, the past of man which each man shares. The elemental dimension of existence, highlighting as it does our identity with nature and our origins in the past, is also an experience of a larger whole than the moments and patches of the temporal present. The two dimensions of the cosmic and the elemental are in this way similar, though the former extends far beyond the nature and scope of the latter. We are citizens both of our lovely planet pulsating with life and the beauty of nature and of the larger cosmos spread in the infinity of space and time. The awareness of this dual citizenship is for me the highest achievement of the human person and the most precious element of the quality of my life. The extension of this personal awareness to a larger awareness shared by my society enriches the social life and adds an essential element to all progress and development. Both the cosmic view and the awareness of the nature and origins of life by individual persons as well as by the larger societies afford the two objectives.

But in the alienation from the temporal state of which I am so acutely aware now these two dimensions are powerless to create except in the realm of the mind and the spirit, and even such creations remain incomplete, often irrelevant. I can relax and ascend, but I am cut off from a certain reality that lives essentially in the moment and finds expression in the routine and strife of daily life. I fear escapism and the irrelevance of personal satisfaction drived from the cosmos and from the elements divorced from the reality of the present moment. No, the temporal present is all-important because it is the only habitation of the cosmic and the elemental that is given to mortals. It is the only moment of consciousness, the past having ceased to be and the future still unborn. The temporal present should always comprehend the point of revelation of the cosmic vision and the awareness of the elemental reality. Any sense of alienation from the temporal present clouds the vision of the cosmos and undermines the relevance of the elemental. We are made to live in all three dimensions at the same time and in some balance and harmony that joins all three. This balance and harmony is the product of human creativity. Therefore, the fullness of life is given to creative persons living harmoniously on all three dimensions of the cosmic, the elemental and the temporal.

Creativity, then, is the power to balance, harmonize and integrate, to be aware of all the parts that make a whole without losing sight of the whole that is far more than its parts, and to be able to live in the intensity of fullness at least in the moments of creation. A sense of harmony, the wholeness of integration and the intensity to know, express and transcend are the three essential hall-marks of creativity. All three operate together, in periods of long labour or prolonged waiting, or in moments of sudden flashes of luminosity, emanating spontaneously from some kind of simmering that had gone on both consciously and unconsciously. The apparent manifestations of the birth of creativity vary widely, depending upon the nature of the creating agent, the object of creation and the integrity and equality of the final creation itself. The achievement of creation is marked by three elements of discovery, uniqueness and communicability.

Some sense of discovery always enters into the creative process. The creator is impelled by an itch or urge to know the unknown and to build what has never existed before. The sense of discovery leads to the creation of something special and unique. The creation may be small and familiar; it is never commonplace and trivial.

The uniqueness of creation lies in the quest of the creator who brings into play the entire uniqueness of his personality, harnessing all its resources in the fullness of the creative effort. Ordinary, routine and commonplace living expresses moments and fragments of thought and action in time and space. Creative living is always in search or transcendence, groping towards meaning and synthesis, defying the limitations of time and place, always achieving some measure of expansion or flight of the spirit in success or failure. A creative act cannot be repeated because its uniqueness has given it a form and a meaning which were born out of circumstances that will never again be the same.

Communicability is the third element of creation. By its very nature the product of creativity is intended for a larger sharing, or the striving to be universal. It is, as it were, an offering of the creater to all creation. That is how God created the universe and the spirit of such a divine creation can be felt by all created things. For us mortals of the human species on a tiny speck of the universe the measure of our creation is infinitely small and insignificant; but the quality and thrust of the creative act partake of that spirit of the divinity from which we ourselves emanated. An element of universality enters into all creation.

But I have wandered off from the main point which was the problem of finding the ways and means of achieving creativity or fullness of life by harmonizing the temporal, which cannot be renounced, with the cosmic and the elemental, which should not be forgotten. Man's frequent sloth and faint-heartedness, and his abiding fear and greed, often employed in the pursuit of false gods of power and wordly values, have so far condemned him to a track of history which has projected prominently only his lower nature, hiding the few beautiful creations of saints, sages and artists among the vast ocean of meaningless, forgotten deeds. Can we reverse this process? Instead of being so sparse and exceptional, cannot creativity be the normal manifestation of human life? I believe such a leap of transcendence to be not only possible, but inevitable if we have to survive as a species and avoid the temptation of committing suicide by senseless violence or sheer decadence. The enormity of the danger and the supreme challenge to human life now posed to all mankind may generate that rare spark of creativity and the upsurge of moral and spiritual resources to keep it alive which are necessary to the blossoming of wisdom, compassion and courage for the attainment of transcendence in an ever-ascending perception and experience of life's meaning and quality. We are moving towards that moment of man's destiny when the choice is narrowed to the shooting at the stars by mobilizing fully the power and potentiality of the inner man and harnessing his physical, intellectual and spiritual energies for new creations of conscious transcendence or perishing in confusion, selfishness, greed and fear with a bang or a whimper.

The continuing
battle of culture

A time for sacrifice

Takeo Kuwabara

There is no doubt about it: our choice must be survival. And what survival if not the survival of human life? But what is human life? There is material life, moral life, cultural life—and so on. Here we are concerned with life pure and simple, with no additional qualification or epithet. For example, when floods brought famine to Bangladesh, the Japanese Unesco Association came to the relief of the victims, but we took no account, in what we did, of their religious, cultural, or even their educational level. All we hoped for was that our help would ensure their survival. Similarly, it is life pure and simple, in other words, physiological life, that we are trying to protect against the threat of nuclear arms; this must be so.

Objectively, every person, as a human being, is equal to all others without distinction. But as an individual, every man is different, whether internally or externally, and his face shows it. The individual can in fact never be satisfied to live at the purely physiological level only. He also has to live at the cultural level, which usually means living the way his ancestors did. It should be noted, however, that although individual differences exist, there are nevertheless elements that are common to a particular group. Every Japanese face, for instance, is different even though, in the streets of Paris, they are all identifiable as Japanese because of a few shared and unvarying traits. Nor should it be forgotten that the one fact explains the other, that every one has his own ways of thinking, indeed of living which are generally characteristic of his country and his cultural sphere.

Normally, the traditional culture peculiar to any cultural
sphere persists unchanged as long as it undergoes no outside
influences. And there are on our planet countless distinctive
cultures. Unesco accepts both the absolute equality of men
as well as their cultural equivalence, which consequently
leads it to respect all cultural particularities too. Unesco
feels that cultural diversity is the prerogative of the whole
human race: a very reasonable stand, but one that is currently under attack. It would therefore be unrealistic to
overlook that fact.

At the dawn of modern times, that is at the time of the
French Revolution, Saint-Just said: 'Happiness is a new
idea in Europe.' The idea that not only the nobility but all
other classes of society—all people—have a right to happiness
and that the pursuit of happiness must be accepted as good
and just, is a European idea. That is true. But it is an idea
that has gradually been propagated throughout the world.
Since mankind first came into being, the potential desire to
satisfy needs has existed. But it has been thwarted by the
inadequacy of productive forces. Aside from a few privileged individuals, most people have had to resign themselves
to want. This unhappy state of affairs changed with the
increase in production due primarily to modern scientific
and technical progress. Saint Just saw it coming: mass
production was born in Europe. And it may be noted in
passing that the same Saint-Just also had the insight to
foresee that colonial powers would one day fall into decline.

I am aware, of course, of the ravages caused by pollution,
and of the fact that there is today, even among scientists,
an 'anti-science'. Yet, since we can no longer abandon the
pursuit of happiness, European-style, we cannot reject
modernization, the means by which this new happiness is to
be achieved. It is true that the Third World countries also
want to share in development and it is becoming harder and
harder to defend the joys of the 'simple life' and the charms
of folk culture. The regions I myself have seen have been
limited to villages in the Himalayan foothills, the Central
African savannah, and the Kingdom of Bhutan, but I am
convinced that the traditional life of the past must change.
I sensed very strongly that the traditional cultures native to
these places harbour elements that run counter to modern
development.

It is very difficult to come out for or against modernization in what might be called philosophical terms.
Whatever may be thought of the decision at an ideal level,
it must be clearly understood that modernization is inevitable: I mean that it must necessarily come to every country

in the present-day world. And if we pursue development through modernization, we must face the inevitability of running counter to tradition. That Japan, which until 1868 had never been a wealthy country, has virtually succeeded in modernizing itself, is due to the fact that is has undergone a very daring 'cultural revolution', directed to that end. I might point out, by the way, that the term 'cultural revolution' was not originated by Mao Tse-tung. It was first employed by Dr Erwin von Bertz, who had come to Japan to teach modern medicine, to describe the Japanese society of the time. The Japanese possessed an ancient tradition, but because of the weak impact of religion, this tradition, with its fragile ideological foundation, remained purely aesthetic. That is the chief explanation for the relative ease with which Japanese tradition was overcome. In the modern State of Japan this tradition continues to survive, but it has been metamorphosed.

That Japan's 'cultural revolution' has its superficial and even negative aspects is true enough, and I have no intention whatsoever of boasting to you about it. Nevertheless, in the cause of development, some extremely elegant old traditions must be modified. In the old Asian countries, for instance, labour has traditionally been held in contempt. In ancient China, for example, the nobility prided themselves on allowing their nails to grow excessively long (it is impossible to do manual work with nails that are too long). It would scarcely be appropriate for the Japanese, whom the whole world accuses of working too hard, to say so. In any case, such traditional ways of thinking must be modified despite the fact that they have existed for so long. 'Interference in internal affairs' is a term which has had a bad press and is hard to accept. Yet if, in order to avoid the disappearance of mankind and live in peace, we admit the need to set up a new human social order and to 'rebuild public morality throughout the world', may I say frankly that we ought to be allowed to declare our opposition to the manufacture of the atom bomb in India. We ought also to be permitted to suggest that, if the Indians would put a stop to overprotecting animals—whether monkeys or cows—the problem of food would be lessened. Obviously I am not saying this as a criticism of India; I cite India simply because it represents one of the oldest civilized countries in Asia and the entire world.

In the present-day world, more than a million people die every year from hunger. That makes a total of a 1,000 million by the year 2000, according to Alfred Kastler's projections. Suppose that the populations of the countries suffering from malnutrition were to ask the glutted nations to get rid of their household pets so as to divert to the starving the food they need. Even though this might be a case of 'interference in internal affairs', the affluent nations could not refuse categorically.

The crisis is serious. To overcome it, we must think only of the unity of mankind. With that in mind, we must not only try to preserve man's cultural heritage, but must learn, rather, to sacrifice some things. 'Individualism' is a virtue of which modern Europe is proud, but we must avoid taking refuge behind it and imposing it on the peoples of the Third World. And should not the East to some extent abandon its ancient tradition of elegance? For the 'survival' of the human race, are we not obliged to bring about a 'new cultural revolution'?

The time of wrath

Oswaldo Guayasamín

Exactly one year ago, in my own contribution on the preservation of cultural identity in our countries, I voiced my scepticism about the intentions of the institutions and individuals who were to carry out the programmes of international bodies. We all know, of course, that a year is too short a period to solve problems of such magnitude, affecting the whole of mankind. But we also know that the frightful machinery set in motion throughout the world has continued to crush an increasing number of countries during the year which has passed since our last meeting. And there is no indication that by the year 2000, that is, tomorrow, this process will have stopped.

Not that we have lost faith in man. The trouble is that, as we gather to talk about man and his destiny as an individual and as a member of a fraternal community, whole cities and countries are still being, or have been, turned into prisons where silence is imposed by walls of fear. I am, of course, speaking of the countries of Latin America.

I know that examples and cases of physical torture and daily crimes are more or less well-known, and that the frequency of such news items may even eventually tire many of those who are not directly affected. But there is another kind of torture and official crime, less visible and less well-known, which aims at the same objective: the destruction of our peoples by means of the destruction of our culture. I am not even going to talk, as I did last time, of the systematic ideological penetration aimed at turning us into consumers of products and concepts created thousands of kilometres away from our countries, but of the total war declared by fascism on culture.

Half the total population of one of the smallest and poorest countries in South America lives outside it, in a neighbouring country. In another small country, the number of political prisoners is, in proportion to the population, the highest in the world. One out of fifty inhabitants has undergone interrogations and other harassments, and one out of a hundred is an informer. Another country, with 5 million inhabitants, whose native population forms almost 80 per cent of the total, has recently imported 150,000 white settlers from the Republic of South Africa—experts in the application of the policy of apartheid. And we are gradually turning into a vast continent of silence: on the one hand, there is the fear of talking and mistrust of all listeners; on the other, the ban on the sale of records and radio broadcasting of folk songs. One of these countries has even forbidden the use of native musical instruments. In several of them, books are burned, newspapers and magazines closed down, and their archives destroyed. Even the teaching of anthropology and sociology is forbidden in some universities. The corpses of teachers and students are found lying in the streets in the morning in many cities in our America. And the crime of the intellectual appears to be so serious that it is not sufficient to torture him, to force him to wander from one country to another, or to kill him: it also frequently happens that children, whatever their age, also have to pay for the crime of thinking.

We have spoken of the cultural genocide at the time of the Spanish Conquest, mentioning the destruction of the unity and the exchanges which existed from Mexico to Patagonia, and the repression of an art and a language. But today, now that we have, over 400 years, built up another type of civilization, the system seems to have grasped that it is the writers and painters, the poets and musicians, the teachers and other bearers of culture, who keep popular memory alive. Hence they try to leave us with no memory of ourselves, they try to induce us to forget what we were and what we are, so that we may not know what we should be. Or so that we may become only what our repressive rulers would like us to be.

I think it is obvious that I am not speaking of an archaeological conception of culture, that I am not referring to those of its values which have become museum pieces, nor to the aspects of folklore intended for tourists. I am speaking of our living culture, of our present way of life, the heir of our previous modes of existence. And those who have not been

'Creative artists spring from the womb of peoples whom they encompass in their works. The Spaniard Picasso reveals African art to the world; the American Calder brings to the fore the mobiles which adorn the houses of the Tao Indians of New Mexico; the Englishman Moore experiments with pre-Columbian forms from Mexico; kinetic art, now universal, with limitless possibilities for development in the remaining part of this century, has roots in tropical Latin America. Hence, the commonly observed gulf separating the work of art from the people is due neither to an élitist attitude on the part of the creative artist, nor to lack of interest on the part of those for whom it is intended, but rather to the barriers set up by those responsible for the dissemination of the work.

'Just as, in admiring the work of Leonardo, we can understand the whole outlook of the Renaissance, so it is the role of the present-day artist to include in his works all that typifies contemporary thought. Each moment in history is characterized by a guiding idea, which may take the form of religion, science or philosophy. I believe that the present time is characterized by man's struggles to find a more human way of life, to build an era in which we are no longer obliged to paint *The Time of Wrath*.

'At the great periods of mankind's artistic creation —whether it be the paintings of the Ajanta caves or the sculptures of Ellora in India, the Egyptian pyramids and the sphinx, or the sculpture and architecture of the Greek temples or Gothic cathedrals—the work may possibly have been conceived by a single man, but, both he and the multitudes who contributed to his achievement had confidence and absolute faith in the survival of their culture. In the present age, by contrast, ferocious individualism and the constant threat that today may be humanity's last, have forced us, the painters, to be the sole creators of our work. If the twenty-first century eventually becomes what we so deeply desire it should be, then new generations will witness the rebirth of art through collective achievement.'—O.G.

imprisoned, tortured, murdered or exiled are subjected to an ideological bombardment inflicted through the mass media for communication—which in our case are media for isolating and dividing—for the benefit of the economic interests of the great centres of power, and, rarely, but very rarely, for the benefit of culture. Furthermore. I would say that these media, and in particular television, really serve as the lethal weapons of peace, as destructive as those of war. And the warlike act of wresting from us our culture is determined by an economic policy which takes no account of the needs of our countries, for the simple reason that it is formulated in the great metropolitan centres of imperialism, and in accordance with their requirements.

I should like to give an example which is, at the same time, an allegory. For our native forebears, gold was the earthly representation of the sun, and the Spanish conquerors converted it, in the eyes of our own peoples, into a source of wealth and power. But the conquest of Quito, the sacred city of the sun, where there is no shadow since it was built in the middle of the world 3,000 years before the arrival of the mounted men, signified for the latter, not only the acquisition of gold, but also the destruction of one of the sacred centres of our culture.

We, the Indian and mixed-blood peoples of the Andean high plateau, have a similar history, our own particular way of life, the same outlook and conception of the world, and a deep desire for brotherhood. We recognize ourselves in our music, in our dances, above and beyond frontiers. But imperialism foments divisions, not only between countries and peoples, in whom it creates nationalist feelings which sometimes turns out to be dangerous: from our childhood on, anger against our neighbours is instilled in us, so that the Indian who was born on this side of the imaginary frontier line is led to hate the Indian born on the other side, and our peoples are manipulated into bawling out a national anthem behind a flag. But the big capitalists, the diabolical alliance of the multinational corporations, and the armies of the great powers have interfered, or are ready to interfere in our affairs, violating all frontiers. Thus, with the destruction of that other sacred element in our culture—our cultural unity—the market for the big arms producers expands, and our rulers fall naïvely, and sometimes fully conscious of the commission they will receive, into the share of acquiring aeroplanes, tanks and other military equipment. And in poor countries like mine, where the figures for illiteracy, infant mortality and malnutrition are appalling, while a fantastic proportion of the national budget goes to the purchase of submarines for war, schoolgirls have to go about the streets asking as it were for alms for the fight against cancer.

Some of this may have been said before, but it is necessary to repeat it. It is true that international conferences are held more and more frequently on the fight against racialism, the preservation of the environment, the pollution of the air, earth and water, the shortage of food and world famine. And in these gatherings, as in regional alliances, the Third World is starting to become aware of its strength, to denounce the exploitation of which it is the victim, and to rediscover and defend its cultural identity.

Unesco has been engaged for several years in one of its noblest tasks: that of reconciling cultural identity with cultural diversity. But unless all the countries in the world are firmly resolved to contribute to this work, not only by increasing the Organization's budget and, for that purpose, reducing their own military expenditure, but also by eradicating the ignominious use of torture and the genocide of intellect, we can cherish few hopes for the year 2000.

I remember that when Luis Echeverría was president of Mexico, he told us in Quito that statesmen, economists, sociologists and politicians should pay great attention to the works of artists, because the latter, by virtue of their intuition or their knowledge, have a deeper insight into the realities of a people's existence. But what is happening in many of our countries, as I said at the beginning, is precisely the opposite: the statesmen of these countries have set themselves to persecute artists and destroy their works, for thinking, feeling and creation have become criminal offences.

I have painted for half a century as if I were crying out in despair. And my cry has joined all the other cries expressing the humiliation and anguish of the age in which we were fated to live. And, despite everything, with the hope of reaching, one day, perhaps in the twenty-first century, the ideal of a world without poverty, hatred or illiteracy. A world in which cultures fashioned by the people as the potter shapes his pitcher are cared for as the peasant lovingly cares for the land and its seed. For our world is small, as the astronauts have seen it from outer space, and should be, as they have also seen it, a world without frontiers, armies, wars, national anthems or flags.

Decolonizing the domain of the spirit

Hephzibah Menuhin-Hauser

There is no doubt that some people, most people maybe, are driven by mounting terrors. We do not know what they are. They may be ill-remembered catastrophes from previous lives which torment their subconscious or these people may have suffered violence at birth, or they may have lost their nerve in childhood, listening to quarrelling parents, or they may have witnessed cruelty so devastating that they grow up afraid to live, afraid to die, and yearning only for temporary relief from unbearable anguish.

But we know enough to know that knowledge of this kind alone cannot help us to change the course of history. We know that wherever there have been great concentrations of human intelligence and organized activity these have led to spectacular achievements, such as the exemplary social revolution in China, or the miracle of space travel, or the regional application of cures for fatal diseases, but only where there has been respect for natural laws and principles and dedicated team-work for a common purpose. These are some of the qualities without which there are no milestones in human progress.

There is a domain, however, in which very little progress has been made and that is in our spiritual world, wherein lies the source of motivation, that secret and invisible place from which flows the will and a double solidarity: the solidarity not only between people who like one another and understand one another and know one another, but the solidarity between ourselves and those who will live after we are dead, to whom and to whose survival our lifespan ought to be dedicated. This is a domain which can claim no success

comparable to the developments brought about by the cure
for polio or the geodesic dome. This spirit space which is
the home of freedom is being filled at the moment with myths
that lead to madness, with hatreds inspired by the virulent
stereotypes perpetuated by history books and our minds, as
well as those of our children, are being continuously pres-
surized and colonized at a faster rate than that at which we
are able to unlearn the falsehoods that we are being daily
taught.

Sean MacBride made reference to the manner in which
multinational and economic interests closely linked to the
industrial–military complex are acquiring and dominating
important organs of the press and thereby seeking to control
our minds and spirits. But our worst enemy is the cynicism
of those who, having tried and failed, cast their gloom on
those who are determined, more than ever, to cultivate the
spirit's freedom, in others and in themselves. Amongst the
people who try to depress are the educators, the psychiatrists,
the economists, the disappointed ex-idealists and other
would-be doctors of social sickness, some of whom continue
to offer tempting cures which are already known to have
failed.

They remind me of the storks I heard of in Israel who
now stand around some automated chicken processing
plants waiting for the offal to be burnt so that they can eat
barbecued chicken all the year round. They no longer need
to migrate because they now live in a welfare State.

Yes, we need more than barbecued chicken to make us
strong enough to fly into the year 2000.

People have a right to think for themselves and to work
at their collective survival and to bypass the threat of atomic
annihilation which is but the symbol of a power game being
played by the ancient and very boring paternalists who are
still trying to prevent people from turning their own creative
ideas into words and songs, and their words and songs into
plans, and their plans into deeds.

The challenge of the year 2000 is none other than the
challenge facing us all—intellectuals, artists and people—
today, to find ways of combating on the one hand corruption
by physical comfort and spiritual apathy, and on the other
hand physical violence and violence to the spirit.

The pieces of information which have been presented to
us so far are lying around in the minds of all of us like
precious, somewhat disjointed components, out of which a
new creation is to emerge. The year 2000 is waiting for our
will to put common purpose into practice. Our various
statements have shown that we all believe basically that

what stands between possible disaster and the hope of survival is nothing more than the free will of people to fight for their life, their way, with the help of creative experts and not led by expert slave-drivers. This people's will is being constantly manipulated and paralysed, and when I say people I include ourselves because our own will to fight is also being constantly threatened and paralysed by references in the mass media, and amongst ourselves, to mass killing—all of this produces, even in us so-called free-thinkers, a feeling of paralysis or cynicism which we simply cannot afford in the midst of battle.

My proposal therefore is that we should establish amongst ourselves a working party. Some of us are near enough to get together in person and those of us who are not may do so by correspondence. And this working party should unite those of us who want to work very specifically at ways of combating manipulation of the mind, by helping people to think their own thoughts and to get together to take their own action. We are well aware of the power struggle of which this manipulation is an essential feature.

The manipulation of anxiety is the first and best weapon of psychological warfare. This is the exact opposite of what has brought us all here together. A natural will to live and to let live which is characteristic of free minds.

A laboratory of life

Jerzy Grotowsky

Culture. What is it after all? A supplement to life, or a factor in life itself? Is it a luxury? It is, of course, often a luxury product. But if it is a question of mental revolution, of moral revolution, then the old formulas are inadequate: what is at stake is a certain way of living. It is true that, beyond what may be called the 'cultural phenomenon', there lie hunger, penury and violence. And the importance of culture, which I believe to be increasing, may have to do with its frailty. Are not all the potentialities of my own life contained therein?

I feel therefore that each of us should pay the closest possible attention to what goes on today in the cultural domain. To speak about what I know, my own field, the theatre, what do I see? People, human beings, interacting simply, freely, within a group—a collective—in which life and creativity are one and the same thing.

There is a need for receptiveness to what exists elsewhere, to let us say what is different from myself, to a culture unlike my own. There is a need for self-assertion through the perfectly tangible expression of a few: for instigating through vital interaction a phenomenon which transcends pure aesthetics, something which cannot be identified as still music or already theatre, as a visual, tangible, object, or as an object already charged with energy. Yes, great culture, culture with a capital C, is and will remain valid. Its maturity cannot be denied. But the culture now taking shape, now being born, fragile and embryonic, is it any less worthwhile? It may be deficient aesthetically. But humanly speaking, it is a major event. How can we make it understandable? It is a kind of reserve, like our forests, a laboratory of life, an incubator. That is something of the utmost importance if you want to link creativity to a way of life. Yes, culture is a certain reflection of reality, it has its collective functions, it is bound up with individuals and peoples in their unique dignity. And it is something more: research, balance, compensation.

During the first phase of industrialization, the Romantic movement developed in Europe. It was as though the excess weight had been moved from one pan of the scales to the other in order to balance it. We have talked at length about life and death, but I should like to talk about something that is being born, something which might so easily be broken.

If our civilization, despite the comforts with which it provides us, leaves such dark clouds hovering over us, it may be because of the notion of immediate utility. Waste itself is a function of immediate utility: we cut wood while it is still green, eat the wheat before it is ripe. But for the future, what seeds of culture ought we to preserve? Perhaps the seed is a product of an encounter among various factors which is not of any immediate use, an encounter in which people rediscover themselves, and others. Take a close look at anyone who is not interested in fame, career or money, but is prompted only by the need to express what he feels. All he wants is to experiment, with himself, with others, with the world, like a village child set free in an orchard. If we cannot slow down the spread of urban civilization—and I believe that it will keep on developing—it is this very urban civilization, with all its artifices and technology, which amplifies the significance of the direct and straightforward meeting of minds that fully validates spontaneous expression in which human values are of more importance than aesthetic ones. As ecology begins to impregnate culture, it becomes obvious to us that the theatre cannot come solely from the division between actors and audience. It has its own pathway to follow; not a highroad; no, it has to clear its own way through the forest.

It is because we wish to escape from urban tyranny that we are making ecology a part of a new culture, that we are seeking a new way of life. There is thus little profit in earning more money, accumulating possessions, extending your personal authority and power or becoming a leader, if you have to die without giving a meaning to life. Those who cut green wood will before long be snuffing out the lives of the young—and the not so young.

Our scorn for others is simply a reflection of our scorn for ourselves. And anyone who believes he is one of God's

elect will some day be asked, 'What have you done on earth?'
It will not be the big things that will count, but the way life
has been lived. I myself feel a profound need for things that
are not profit-oriented, for things that can restore to me a
child's wisdom and understanding; which can help me see
things as a child sees them, touch them as a child does. The
knowledge of the emergent culture is the child's knowledge
and the sage's. If anything has been granted me in my
experience which I can perceive as a sudden insight, a
glimmer of light that I can use as a guide, two words come
to my mind which are, for me, inseparable and make sense
as a pair: 'clarity' and 'wonder'.

Building for tomorrow

Bernard Zehrfuss

1 In 1933, an assembly of the International Congresses for Modern Architecture (ICMA) was held in Athens. ICMA was founded in 1928 by a group of architects who had met in Switzerland to decide what the real function of architecture was. Conscious of the profound upheavals caused by mechanization, they recognized that changes in the social structure and the economic order inevitably produce corresponding changes in the phenomenon of architecture. The Athens congress, their fourth, was devoted to a study of thirty-three cities and to the drawing up of a Town-planning Charter. Eight years later, in 1942, a book entitled *La Charte d'Athènes* was published anonymously in Paris, revealing the existence of this document to the public. The ninety-five recommendations of the Charter were accompanied by notes written by Le Corbusier. A second edition of this work, with various additions to the Charter made by Le Corbusier, was published in 1957 by Editions de Minuit (Paris).

If we were to give the architect's social function full play by freeing it from the constraints of vested interest and speculation, we might then be able to build beautiful cities for people to be happy in.

Such a social function means social change, of course, and presupposes that nations, having stopped their frenzied arms race, will begin thinking about the background to their citizens' lives and call on them to restore its quality.

It might be a good idea to begin with a review of the mistakes made over the past fifty years so as to learn from them for the good of future generations.

I have often spoken out against the destruction of towns and villages, and magnificent sites, caused by the total lack of any town-planning philosophy and by the spread of a kind of all-purpose architecture which has invaded not only Europe but all the other continents as well. Today I speak out against those who dare to talk about the environment and at the same time allow polluting factories and atomic power plants to be installed near where people live without the slightest thought for humanity.

People must combine their efforts to put an end to such criminal chaos; the quality of life we hear so much about must force the authorities to apply certain elementary rules which will constitute the basis for tomorrow's society.

I have already referred to the part that Unesco could play here: I cited the example of the International Congress of Modern Architects, which courageously set forth some major architectural and town-planning principles in the famous Athens Charter.[1]

It appears that a new charter dealing with housing might now be drawn up, and not only by architects.

We shall still have to build homes for people. In this context, I have said that we might rely on architects, but they still have to be prepared for the task. Current architectural training in almost every country in the world ends up with the same forms of expression, the same formulas, bastardized forms of those which derive from the architectural revolution at the beginning of this century in Europe. Such forms of expression take no account of the diversity of cultures, or of the traditions peculiar to each region, or of individual ways of life, or of adaptation to particular sites.

Thus in the universities and schools of America, Africa and Asia, students learn the same forms and adopt the same architectural idioms as in Europe. The fact that architecture is the reflection of a variety of civilizations, that its richness lies in its diversity, is overlooked. In another sphere, it is also forgotten that architecture must not give in to technology but control it.

Unesco has a part to play too, in directing such training and promoting the education of those who, in a few years time, will be called on to build this new face of the world, with the object of making it not only beautiful and harmonious but uplifting as well. For architecture is creative imagination, and, while retaining our mastery of the immense technological possibilities now open to us, we can invent new forms of astonishing daring, each of them different, depending on their surroundings, and capable of giving back to people something they have lost: the passion and zest for life.

The right
to a vocation

Alicia Penalba

As the human race is steadily increasing, it is perhaps time to begin worrying about the increase in human foolishness fostered by the greed of cultural drug pedlars.

Their future customers are the children born today who will be 22 in the year 2000, and I am horrified at the thought that, unless we come up with another system for introducing them to life, the quality of individuals will turn out to be ten times worse than it is today, and the mistakes of the past ten times more serious.

We hear a lot about the quality of life, but seldom anything about the quality of individuals. The distortion of instinct, of the sensitivity and tenderness we all possess at birth, weighs heavily on our consciences.[1] It is repeated *ad nauseam* that 'Art is the essential good in life', but I, personally, have an indelible memory of the problems I had in getting rid of the cultural vices with which I had been inoculated. Later on, in art schools, I noticed that the students who were not strong enough to protect themselves from the authoritarianism of the teachers were unable subsequently to resist the temptation of banality in industrial art.

Those who took advantage of their weaknesses took over their dreams, their souls, their personal independence. The money-changers are in control of the temple, and the creative, domesticated by inferior teaching, is directed towards a culture of industrial consumerism whose portals are invariably ornamented with a cash-register.

Few indeed are those (one in 10,000, perhaps) who survive this mystification and become aware of true freedom,

1 'No, no!' said the Queen. 'Sentence first—verdict afterwards.' 'Stuff and nonsense!' said Alice loudly. 'The idea of having the sentence first!'—Lewis Carroll *Alice's Adventures in Wonderland.*

the freedom to choose their own culture, decide their own lives and restore themselves to the condition of human beings. More than ever, in fact, I feel that art is not a luxury but that it has become a luxury and must cease to be such.

History testifies to the fact that man has never done without art. Art is already present in the universe of the child. Today, however, it might be wiser not to talk about the situation as regards art and adults.

It has been said that art is élitist. I personally think this is an untenable position. If art implies élitism and the star system, if it is to be enclosed in specialists' ghettos, it is because art is increasingly in revolt against society and the symbols it resorts to are ever more abstract, philosophical and difficult to decipher. Only initiates, with the time to study them at their leisure, can deal with such enigmas and end up understanding them. Most people, however, work eight hours a day and do not have the time to investigate any subject whatsoever. Of course, there are more and more museums throughout the world, and we are more and more concerned with art. But the man in the street does not go to museums and does not understand scholarly debate. None of it is important. And for the child things are even worse: museums are monuments to boredom, and a visit to the museum is a punishment. Where are the museums for children? We have to create them, many of them. They would contain toys from all over the world, of every period, with reproductions of a great variety of works of art: African dolls, true works of art, and little pre-Columbian sculptures to develop a feeling for form and colour. The universe of games as original creations would unfold before their eyes. Children must be encouraged to discover, invent and choose for themselves. They must be trained to insist on quality. In that way their taste and thought will be shaped.

A culture flourishes through the free expression of emotion, the practice of such expression, and awareness that 'doing' is a marvellous source of happiness.

The illnesses of adult life must be warded off from the start of existence: we are all the products of our childhood. The child imitates, and he imitates his parents first of all. Perhaps we ought to set up schools for parents. In 1959, the United Nations adopted a declaration of the rights of the child.[2] It deals with a variety of questions but says nothing about the vocation of the child, the respect this vocation ought to inspire and the child's rights of access to creativity. All this seems basic to me. Most parents cannot understand the aspirations of their children, who grow up frustrated and alienated.

2 On 20 November 1959, the United Nations General Assembly unanimously adopted the Declaration of the Rights of the Child. The Preamble affirms that 'mankind owes to the child the best it has to give'. A number of rights and freedoms had already been proclaimed in the 1948 Universal Declaration of Human Rights, but the international community was convinced that the needs of the child required a special declaration. This contains ten Principles which explicitly state the rights that a child should be universally recognized as having. The right to a vocation may be considered implicit in Principle 2 which stipulates that the child must be in a position 'to develop physically, mentally, morally, spiritually and socially in a healthy and normal manner and in conditions of freedom and dignity'.

A narrow, self-centred conception of the family does not bode well for human relationships later on. It is in play that learning to live begins. Play is a preparation for life in society; it opens the way to a liking for life in society. Places are therefore needed where the child can discover the world and himself (it might be better not to call them museums): rich, open, non-limiting collections where the child can discover what he cannot find at home and indeed the exact opposite of what he discovers there through television—vulgarity, violence and money. Poor children are daily traumatized by adult tragedies and most children are poor. Too many, children are still martyred by parents who use them only as pretexts for working out their own fears and difficulties. Shall we ever be able to do away with the iniquity and violence born of simmering family grudges?

If adults have any confidence in mankind, let them restore to children the power to decide their own vocation, their culture and their destiny. They will then discover what beauty is.

The risk of
the lowest common
denominator

Schuyler Chapin

In my recent days as General Manager of the Metropolitan
Opera in New York, I was once accused by an irate maestro
during an artistic crisis of being a commissar of optimism.
This was meant pejoratively, of course, but it also happens
to reflect what I feel. If one begins to think seriously, as
we here all do, of the frightening dangers of the future,
especially as we race toward the year 2000, the seeming sense
of impasse that so much of our thinking is stressing can make
us feel that we might as well go home and pull the blankets
over our head until the apocalypse comes. Let us consider
the arts; where, for instance, they fit into our risky future.
The arts are, after all, in the words of novelist Katherine
Anne Porter, what we leave behind when cities fall, and
almost since the dawn of time they have been the signature
of man. As history unfolds it is the arts that are man's
permanent record, not the battles or the flags of the monuments. We have only to look at Egypt, at Greece, at Rome,
among many others, to underscore that fact, and there is
nothing in our turbulent world today that in any way
indicates that this truth is changing. But what about the
arts now, as a living part of our age? Do we not sense that
something is happening here, something that could be an
optimistic sign that all is not lost? We know for a fact that
in the present society of the West, there is enormous eager-
ness to embrace the arts, almost as an antidote to the
increasing plastic conformity of our present lives. In many
socialist States there may be indifference to official painting
and sculpture, but in the performing arts, especially in the
theatre, major changes and developments have taken place

in countries such as Yugoslavia, and particularly Poland where eighteen short years brought about a highly controversial but major breakthrough in theatrical conception. And look at the Paris Opera, for years an international joke and now, almost the leading company of the world. Have you tried to see the new Beaubourg Museum? Twenty-five thousand people a day try to do so, the building almost groans under their weight. And so it is in galleries and concert halls and opera houses and theatres all over the world. The opportunities for artists have never been better, and what is even more important, the public is demanding higher and higher standards. I submit to you that there are no real, no genuine talents starving in garrets these days. There may be some whose talents are simply not good enough, who put on a good show about being denied opportunity but for the most part this is a cover-up for their own inadequacies. No, at this particular moment, the creative surge of art is strong. The work of artists often reflects the disabilities of our own societies, they paint us in various, often torturous ways. Sometimes we stand appalled at what is being written by our poets and playwrights and novelists, painted by our painters, played by our musicians, sung by our singers, danced by our dancers, but few can deny the vigour and passions that guide these talented people, and few remain untouched by their outpourings. They are truly the signatures of our age. But what about the twenty-three-odd years ahead before the beginning of the twenty-first century? Will the present vigour be maintained? Or will art like so much of contemporary life, fall victim to our increasing denial of excellence, our willingness to allow shoddy workmanship and ideas to dominate our cultures? As we move steadily into the future, what are we going to do with the increasing leisure time that new scientific advances have endowed people with everywhere? It might be wonderful if Buckminster Fuller's Utopian dream of a world where there was no longer any need of work became a reality. But what would people do then to fill up their lives? I submit that one of the major areas that will be affected by these changes will be the arts, not that the arts are necessarily for everyone. At the risk of incurring your grave displeasure, I venture to suggest that the arts are essentially aristocratic, even—that dreadful word—élitist. But aristocratic and élitist in the sense that they demand interest, curiosity, involvement on the part of their creators, their re-creators and their audience. All these forces must meet and present evidence would seem to indicate that this is occurring in an exciting and, I believe, crucial way. But it is essential that standards be preserved. We must not fool ourselves into thinking that the participation of large numbers of people in the arts is *per se* the answer. We must use all the communications technology at our disposal to see that the arts are exposed to as many people as possible, but we must be careful not to play down to the lowest common denominator. We must encourage all signs of interest and involvement as they appear throughout the years. Thank God we live in a world where the arts are as varied as our multi-cultures. We must continue to see to it that the variety is strengthened and that the individual is given a sense of the meaning of his or her particular culture and artistic traditions.

Music is vulnerable too

Tran Van Khe

It is hardly surprising, seeing that mankind remains un-
concerned by the problem of its own survival, that it should
also be indifferent to the decline and extinction of some
musical traditions. When it was a matter of rescuing
Egyptian monuments, saving Venice from drowning or
restoring ancient remains, world opinion was aroused and
tremendous efforts of every kind were deployed. But nobody
seems to realize that a type of music can become extinct, or
that it is a very fragile work of art, just as worthy of being
rescued as the Egyptian statues and palaces or Angkor Wat.
For nearly twenty years now I have been concerned about
this problem of the disappearance of musical traditions.

I have continually stressed the need to preserve great
musical traditions which are in danger of disappearing,
decried the tendency for European-style music to become
standard in Asia and Africa and for musical traditions
everywhere to become deculturized, and championed the
preservation of cultural identity. It was not until June 1977
that a conference was held, which I attended, to draw up a
ten-year plan for the preservation and advancement of music
and the performing arts in Asia and Africa and to discuss
the technical methods and the ways and means for achieving
this aim. If we go on doing nothing, there is very little time
left before the year 2000 to save many kinds of traditional
music—they will simply disappear. A number of masters
who hold the secrets of an ancient art have already departed,
and more will inevitably do so. And in Asia and Africa,
with the death of a master, a tradition often dies out, a
library disappears. For that reason, I have no compunction

about reverting to the problem of preserving musical traditions.

To speak of preservation implies that something is endangered, and also that the thing to be preserved has a certain value. I should therefore like to consider very briefly the factors which bring about the disappearance of traditions.

The main factor is political, namely colonization. Political colonization brought with it cultural colonization, which sought to impose an alien culture and led to the phenomenon of cultural alienation. This in turn brought with it other consequences on the psychological level, for the colonized seek at all costs to imitate the colonizers, and mistake technology for cultural superiority. Asian and African peoples often forget that it takes only twenty years to train a good engineer, whereas it takes 100 years to build up a culture. That is why they have neglected their most precious asset, which has stood the test of time, in order to try to imitate those who have taken them over by force. This has given all Asian and African musicians an inferiority complex ('all' may be something of an exaggeration, but I think it is true of most). The proof is that, when a student goes to music school, he is proud to show off his violin, whereas when he is learning to play the two-stringed hurdy-gurdy he hides it as though he were ashamed of the instrument.

Traditional musicians may also have a superiority complex, holding that the young people of today are incapable of taking over their tradition from them because they are already corrupted by the West. It is the combination of these two complexes—inferiority on the part of those who need to study, and superiority on the part of those who are competent to teach—that has brought about the decline and, I am very much afraid, the extinction of some musical traditions. Of course, many musical genres have disappeared with the advance of technology. Singing is no longer to be heard in the paddy-fields or where people work, as a result of mechanization. No doubt it is a good thing that men and women should be replaced and liberated by machines; but we must face the fact that the installation of, for instance, husking machinery means the immediate end of all rice-pounding, corn-pounding and millet-pounding songs. I should like to emphasize another psychological factor: laziness, a disease of our time. This is the laziness referred to by Tewfik Al-Hakim, when he deplored the fact that man allowed himself to be supplanted by machines, and it is found on every hand. There is laziness in composition, laziness as regards creative work. Musicians improvise less and less.

Peasants less and less improvise songs as they work: they prefer to listen to other people singing, or even to the radio or records. It is the same in the West. People nowadays think twice about going to concerts, preferring to shut themselves up in their living-rooms and listen through the intermediary of highly sophisticated reproduction equipment to music performed with technical (and possibly artistic) perfection. But this is music deep-frozen, not a live performance. The same laziness is to be found in the realm of religion. I was amazed, and smiled a little sadly, to find that in some Buddhist temples in South-East Asia, the priests no longer recite the prayers. They are recorded once and for all; at prayer-time the priests start the hi-fi equipment, and it reproduces the prayers. The priests do not even bother to go through the motions of moving their lips, but are content to fan themselves even while they listen to the prayers. So it is not only musicians who are smitten with laziness, but also monks, who not only have a religious message to convey but at the same time perform a type of religious music which is tending nowadays to disappear in that part of the world.

Social and economic factors are also contributing to this decline. Those who learn traditional music are sometimes destined to die of starvation, whereas those who learn Western music have no difficulty in getting jobs in tea-houses and night-clubs. This in itself again represents a threat to genuine musical traditions. Yet these traditions are of rare value. There is value also in the instruments used, and in the various materials used in making them. Whereas, in the West, wood, metal and skins are used, in the East stone, wood, metal, silk, gourds and skins of all kinds are employed: not only cowhide but buffalo hide, lambskin and even the skin of foetal lambs, which is used to make the drumskin of the Iranian *tar*. There is not only the beauty and graceful shape of the instruments but the richness of intervals and scales and the multitudinous different modes: the Indian *raga*, the Iranian *dastgah*, the *maqam* of the Arab countries, the Vietnamese *dien*, the *patet* in Indonesia, and so on. These types of music are doomed to extinction unless solutions can be found as a matter of urgency.

First of all, the developing countries must be given material to enable them to become aware of their cultural identity. Let me give an example of what I mean. A research worker from the French Centre National de la Recherche Scientifique (National Scientific Research Centre) went to the Solomon Islands to try to make a collection of traditional music. A couple of months later he wrote to the centre to say that he wanted to come home. 'Everybody here', he wrote, 'plays modern music: they have electric guitars and accordions.' His headquarters begged him to be patient and pursue his search in the hill country. One day he came upon an old musician playing pan-pipes, a type of flute with seven pipes and a scale obtained by dividing the octave into seven equal parts. The research worker wanted to record him, but the old man said: 'This is old-fashioned music; it is not worth it, it is out of date. Record the young instead.' The research worker pressed the point, and the old man thereupon declared that he could not play on his own: 'I must call some of my friends, for it takes four to play.' This was done, and the research worker recorded the four old musicians playing pan-pipes and made a record which was issued in France. He used his royalties to buy record-players and records, which he presented to the people of the Solomon Islands. The prestige of these records brought all the way from France persuaded the young people to listen to this old-fashioned music; and so struck were they by it that many of them have since given up the electric guitar and taken to playing pan-pipes.

So sometimes it takes very little to make a people aware of its culture. Material help certainly plays a big part, and I am very glad to hear that Unesco is working on a ten-year plan for the preservation and advancement of music and the performing arts in the countries of Asia and Africa.

What also needs doing is to cure Asian and African musicians of their inferiority complex by getting top-class traditional musicians invited abroad. They would go home again with their prestige greatly enhanced by having taken part in international congresses or festivals; they would be recognized as masters, and from then on would be able to teach, for the young would be willing to sit at their feet and submit to long years of apprenticeship in the hope of one day equalling them and themselves winning international acclaim.

Lastly, I should like to say a few words about the new cultural revolution. What is needed is a mental revolution, by which I mean that people's way of thinking needs changing as well as the system of teaching music in the West and everywhere else in the world. It is a disgrace that hardly any Western academy teaches Chinese or Indian music, whereas Western music is taught in any academy in Asia or Africa.[1] Furthermore, the history of music needs to be rewritten. When I was asked to write about musical traditions in the Far East, namely China, Japan, Korea, Mongolia and the Socialist Republic of Viet Nam—a whole world—I was allowed only 400 lines, whereas over 1,000 lines were reserved

1 In the United States, courses in 'non-Western music' used to be given at the Institute of Ethnomusicology, University of California, Los Angeles (UCLA). (At the present time, the institute is part of the Department of Music, and the number of hours devoted to the teaching of the music of Asia and Africa has been reduced.) In Europe, there is not one conservatory offering courses in Asian and African music as such. An occasional lecture is given here and there on the musical traditions of the countries of Asia.

for J. S. Bach alone.[2] The history of music, after all, is not the history of Western music, but of the music of the whole world. Next, radio and television programmes need to be reorganized. During the Vietnamese war, it was quite common for pictures of that war to be shown to an accompaniment of Cambodian music. Even though for Western audiences Vietnamese music and Cambodian music are one and the same, the two draw from completely different traditions. I once listened to a programme on France Culture about Chinese civilization: the topic was Peking duck, and it was accompanied by some Vietnamese background music which I know well (having played it myself) and which expresses a mood of serenity. Nowadays, admittedly, such absurdities no longer happen, but we still do not have the kind of radio programme that would serve as a window opening on Asia and Africa. Nothing has been done in this direction, and in France, for instance, France Musique broadcasts traditional music only after midnight. There certainly are people who listen to it, but they must be very few.

Another revolution is called for in the education of the public and the fostering of international cultural contacts. This means contacts not only between Europe and Asia and Europe and Africa but between different regions of Asia and between Asia and Africa, and indeed between neighbouring countries in the same continent. For it is perfectly possible in any Asian or African country to be familiar both with one's own kind of music and with Western music, but to know nothing of the musical scene in neighbouring countries. Otherwise, by around the year 2000, many musical traditions will have become extinct, and laziness will have become the order of the day, destroying all creative urge. We are already in the era of easy living, with pieces easy to compose, easy to write out, easy to remember and easy to forget. Music that calls for concentration is rejected, just as the idea of learning an instrument that takes ten years to master is rejected. If nothing is done, by around the year 2000, variety and originality will have given way to uniformity and standardization, and men will have been replaced by machines. Music will have lost its artistic quality and become nothing but a commercial commodity; and cultural and educational organizations both private and governmental, national and international, will bear the responsibility for an irreparable loss to the whole of mankind.

2 An allusion to the section on 'Histoire de la Musique Orientale', in *La Musique, les Hommes, les Instruments, les Œuvres* (Larousse, 1965).

Personalizing
the message

Paolo Grassi

Among the data on the strength of which we compile and continually revise our forecasts of the shape of things to come in the twenty-first century, there are some purely technical facts regarding global telecommunication by satellite which suggest a whole series of ideas about the future of mankind and the challenge of the year 2000. It is only twelve years since the launching of *Early Bird*, the first commercial telecommunications satellite, and already the use of space for this purpose has grown from one small satellite with a design capacity of 240 bidirectional telephony circuits to an integrated network of eight satellites in orbit over the Atlantic, the Pacific and the Indian Ocean and providing ninety-five nations on the six continents with a total design capacity of 40,000 circuits. Already there are plans to launch a new series of satellites in 1979, each with double the design capacity of the existing ones (12,000 circuits as against 6,000). In the last issue of the Italian edition of *Scientific American*, an article by Burton J. Edelson, Director of Laboratories of the United States Communications Satellite Corporation (COMSAT), gives a full account both of INTELSAT, which is bringing in Mondo Vision, and of possible developments in the short-term future.[1] A diagram in the same article shows the planisphere of our planet almost completely covered by the satellite network. The increasing pace of technological change is too obvious a fact to need restating here but to my mind this state of affairs has serious hidden implications. It means, first of all, that a world-wide telecommunications system already exists, and will continue to grow until it forms

1 This is a reference to the article that appeared in the February 1977 issue of *Scientific American* entitled 'Global Satellite Communications'. Accompanied by maps and diagrams, this study surveys the development of satellite communications since *Early Bird* was launched twelve years ago.

a gigantic network completely covering the globe. (I use the word 'cover' rather than 'unite' advisedly: the latter possibility is something that depends entirely on us.) This network at present consists of permanent telephone, telegraph and data-transmission services, plus special intermittent television channels, mainly commercial, plus (to a lesser extent) programmes whose international character is only apparently neutral and harmless, as for instance the programmes on the Olympic Games.

But the time is coming, will inevitably come, when the system will be used to transmit messages that are not purely utilitarian: there will be information and news programmes, cultural and entertainment programmes. The question then arises: what kind of information and news, what sort of cultural and entertainment programmes? Have we still got time to think about this, or has the consumption machine (and if I may say so, man's mania for self-destruction) long since started to draw up blueprints for these future transmissions, designed to unite peoples of different races, creeds and levels of development under the all-embracing banner of conformity and escapism? Perhaps it is already too late for us radically to rethink the aims and general object of this gigantic telecommunication network, which for the moment exists only academically, but will shortly enclose us completely. We were similarly late in working out the aims and overall purpose of radio: it had already been in use for nearly ten years before public programmes were started. It seems to be almost a general rule that each generation of technologists is surprised and overtaken by the innovations it has itself produced—like the sorcerer's apprentice, unleashing forces which before along they can neither understand nor control. Failing some serious thought by everyone, the danger is that a dense communications network may grow up which will mean only manipulated news and mindless entertainment; or, worse still, the fulfilment of Adorno's warning [2] that continual technological progress could go hand in hand with the continual regression of mankind. An example is the fanatical nationalism of the audience at the Olympic Games, which are supposed, on the contrary, to serve the cause of peace. That is the kind of spectacle which is already relayed by satellite over a large part of the earth's surface. The popularity of the Games is really symbolic of Western paganism, for they celebrate the pagan hero, i.e. the Victor, the strongest one, the one who dominates others. The mixture of commercialism and advertising that is a feature of the modern imitation of the Greek Olympic Games is entirely secondary.

2 A statement reminiscent of A. N. Whitehead, who wrote: 'The major advances in civilization are processes that all but wreck the societies in which they occur.'

For the moment, however, there is not only the INTELSAT network, the satellite telecommunication system that provides high-quality, reliable, profitable telephone and data-transmission services. There is also another much less impressive network which is, however, much more important for us, and that is the network of the world's intellectuals —writers, artists, scientists, scholars, poets, essayists and philosophers. Though scattered all about the earth, they now speak a common language: the language of freedom, born of ingrained independence of mind and resistance to all forms of violence and abuse of power. Their voice is still weak, for as Freud rightly emphasized in *The Future of an Illusion*,[3] the voice of the intellect is weak; but it keeps on until it is heard, and in the end, after innumerable rebuffs, it is. And the primacy of the intellect, if it be an 'undoubted' illusion, at least let me think so as a man of the theatre who has been a lifelong doubter—which is why I so much appreciated Brecht's *Galileo*—may be for a remote future, but perhaps not as remote as all that.

What I mean here is the primacy not of an arrogant intellect, overriding human feelings and emotions, but of a creative intellect. This is one of the problems we need to think about at present: how to co-opt creative minds, representing a true intellectual and artistic élite, on to the councils of the powerful bodies which will have to decide what news and what programmes the satellite network is to broadcast to the world. If the voices of wisdom and truth can make themselves heard in these councils, one of the main topics to be debated will be the grafting of our legacy of humanism on to the most advanced aspects of science. The only people competent to tackle this task are people convinced that, beyond human divisiveness, there is a deep-rooted cohesive urge, and that we are all united by a common humanity far stronger than any unity of dogma; people who realize that the centrifugal forces that have driven mankinds apart must be replaced by integrative structures and processes capable of giving meaning and purpose to life; people aware of the possibility that science itself may, through the limitations of its own methodology, expose mankind to an unpredictable sequence of unimaginable consequences. Werner Heisenberg, the great German physicist and founder of quantum mechanics, used to say that modern science provides a demonstration of the fact that science cannot exist without humanism. Atomic physics, according to him, is the end-result of a culture that started with Plato's *Timaeus*, Democritus [4] and Leucippus and continued with Max Planck. It is the latest extension of a natural philosophy

3 In *The Future of an Illusion* (1927), Freud discusses the question of religious illusion as opposed to science which, although compartmentalized and subject to error, is always capable of rectifying its mistakes and progressing. He concluded: 'No, our science is no illusion. But an illusion it would be to suppose that what science cannot give us we can get elsewhere.' This look at the future is pursued with *Civilization and Its Discontents* (1930).

4 The physics of Democritus (*c.* 420 B.C.) is the first corpuscular physics. He adopted certain hypotheses of Leucippus whose cosmogony was conceived of as an infinite mass from which came the matter of innumerable successive or simultaneous worlds. For a world to be created, it was sufficient for a fragment to break from the mass and be propelled by a whirling movement. On to Leucippus's physics, Democritus grafted the doctrine of atoms, saying that the infinite mass is made up of an infinity of invisible and indivisible corpuscles. Describing the origin of the world, the Pythagorean Timaeus (in the *Timaeus* by Plato), sees in the cosmos a perceptible compound, i.e. a mixture ordered by fixed relationships. It was in 1900 that Planck put forward the theory of the discrete nature of energy and defined quanta.

that bridges the gap between the ancient world and ourselves.

In his attempt to find a formula to cover the whole field, Heisenberg used the units of measurement of modern physics together with hypotheses based on Plato.

It must be repeatedly stressed that as the great communication media expand they become correspondingly more complex: they become mass media, and as they lose touch with the individual, i.e. with the creative capacity and the needs of the individual (which are different from those of the mass), they lose their moral quality. The technological empires themselves, rather like State bureaucracies, feed on themselves, with utter disregard for creativity, which is compelled to conform to their Procrustean modules.

We must plan to reverse this trend. We must make use of technological progress, which gets simpler every day, to enrich mankind in a real sense by encouraging all forms of creativity, and in particular the creativity of the group or community and of the individual within the group.

The personalizing of the message is the ambitious goal we must set ourselves. We cannot hope to meet the challenge of the year 2000 without successfully countering the danger of the mass tendency and progressive standardization inherent in television; and the way to counter this threat is by fostering regard and respect for what is different. This must be a conscious choice which all of us, as responsible educated persons, must make, if we do not want to see the men and women of the future turn into so many cybernetic tortoises, equipped with sensory organs but without a thought in their heads. Diversity is the spice of life, and guarantees our perpetual enrichment and renewal.

The 'third culture', which that great man of the theatre, Peter Brook, told us about last year, also comes into it. Diversity is impossible without tolerance—an important fact which needs to be borne in mind especially by the loyal and arrogant champions of the Eurocentric view. Let us not, however, be too quick to embrace the opposite view, namely that our civilization is doomed to perish and nothing we can do can save it. We need to develop a new international consciousness; a new attitude to nature based on harmony rather than conquest; a new interest in languages, the plurality of cultures, minorities and other ethnic groups; and a sense of identification with future generations. Cross-fertilization with different civilizations and cultures—of which I have some experience in another field, the theatre—will help to make us more aware of our identity with men and women who share the same problems, the same anxieties and the same hopes as ourselves. This is a way of rediscovering in diversity a truer unity.

Moreover modern man, who knows what the earth looks like when viewed from outer space, is returning to his old geocentric position: the astronomical revolution of Copernicus has been followed by the spiritual revolution of Ptolemy. The isolation of the planet Earth now stares us in the face: but with this awesome but necessary thought there comes another, namely that the earth is a holy and infinitely precious place, and that consequently everything, including tremendous scientific and technological advances like telecommunications satellites, must be placed at the service of man—not to overwhelm him as an individual in the mass, but to awaken him and make him realize that he must rediscover himself before disaster strikes.

I have a feeling nowadays that there is something in mankind which will stand up to the threat of an anonymous, amorphous mass culture. It is a new, though often indefinable, inner conviction of the unity of mankind and the world, founded on a sense of the sanctity of the individual and respect for cultural diversity.

I should like to end these few remarks with what I was saying recently about the relationship between the theatre and society: 'Paradise for theatre people is a dialectical society in a state of inner tension, such as Periclean and Elizabethan society may have been.' Society nowadays, in my view, is anything but necessarily monolithic or uniform. It can, indeed it must, be infinitely diversified; but in the last analysis it must have a cohesiveness all its own, a goal all its own to aim at, and a unity and an ethic all its own. These things seem to me to be completely lacking both in Italy and elsewhere in Europe. Yet I do not see the present as a situation beyond repair. On the contrary, I think it is a fascinating time for anyone with vitality and hope. It is not the doldrums, but a storm at sea: the waves may engulf us, and if we think in terms of individual salvation we are lost. But if we can rediscover agreement on the principles that matter, and our love of what we have in common, and if we aim for the salvation of all, then we shall save ourselves as individuals—and also as men of the theatre, educated people and responsible citizens.

Biographical notes

LÉON BOISSIER-PALUN. Member of the Executive Board of Unesco, and a senior member of the Paris bar. Began his political career in Africa during the period of French administration of his country, Benin, continuing until it achieved complete independence. Played an outstanding part in the establishment of new African States.

TRYGVE BRATTELI. Norwegian statesman, has been Finance Minister, Minister for Communications, and twice Prime Minister. Has taken part in numerous international activities, in particular as a member of the Nordic Council.

SCHUYLER CHAPIN. General Manager of the Metropolitan Opera in New York from 1972 to 1975. Since 1976 Dean of the School of Arts at Columbia University, New York.

LUIS ECHEVERRIA ALVAREZ. Mexican Ambassador to Unesco, and President of Mexico from 1970 to 1976. A lawyer, he has been Professor of Political Science at the University of Mexico, and is currently President of the Centro de Estudios Economicos y Sociales del 3er. Mundo, an international institute which conducts social and economic studies on the developing world.

ANDRÉ FONTAINE. Editor of the French daily *Le Monde* since 1969, contributes to a number of overseas publications and foreign broadcasting corporations; in addition to numerous articles, special reports and interviews, he has written several works dealing with international political problems, such as *Histoire de la Guerre Froide*, *La Guerre Civile Froide* and *Le Dernier Quart de Siècle*.

BUCKMINSTER FULLER. An American engineer whose technological innovations, for instance the geodesic dome, have overthrown traditional ideas in building construction. Has held appointments in various universities and technological institutes throughout the world, has been awarded thirty honorary degrees, and is the author of numerous works such as *Utopia or Oblivion (The Prospects for Humanity)* (1960), and *The Buckminster Fuller Reader* (1970).

PAOLO GRASSI. Has been for twenty-five years the Director of the Piccolo Teatro, which he set up in 1947. From 1972 to 1976 was Director of the Teatro alla Scala in Milan, and has collaborated with various publishers in editing drama collections.

JERZY GROTOWSKY. Theatre director and dramatic art teacher. His laboratory-theatre and investigations into a new relationship between the actor and the public have gained him a prominent position in present-day drama, both in Poland and abroad.

OSWALDO GUAYASAMIN. Ecuadorian painter and sculptor. His first major exhibition in 1952, 'Huacaynan' (The path of tears), held in the Colonial Art Museum in Quito, contained 300 paintings. In 1957 was awarded the prize for the best South American painter at the São Paulo biennial festival. Produced large-scale mosaics for the Government Palace in Quito ('The Discovery of the Amazon') and the University of Quito ('The History of Mankind and Culture'). In 1971 designed the monument commemorating the 150th anniversary of the independence of Guayaquil (Ecuador).

TEWFIK AL-HAKIM. Egyptian playwright and novelist, and one of the greatest living Arabic writers. Drew on his experience as a magistrate for *The Magistrate's Diary*; other well-known works are *The Confused Sultan*, *Scheherezade*, *Pygmalion*, *The Cave-Dweller*, *You Who are Climbing the Tree*, *Solomon the Wise*, *Bird of Lebanon* and *Fate of a Cockroach*.

HAN SUYIN. A doctor, who has studied in Peking, Brussels and London. Very widely known as an essayist and novelist, she has aroused a lively interest in the West for Asia today.

PAUL-MARC HENRY. Chairman of the Development Centre of the Organization for Economic Co-operation and Development (OECD) from 1972 to 1977. Has held high positions in economic affairs, both at French national level and in a number of international organizations. Between 1952 and 1957 was a Visiting Fellow at Nuffield College, Oxford. Has taught at the University of California in Los Angeles (UCLA) and is the author of a general history of Africa, *Africa Aeterna*.

MICHIKO INUKAI. A Japanese writer who concentrates on the study of civilizations and the role of Christianity in the world today.

MICHEL JOBERT. *Conseiller-Maître* at the French Cour des Comptes. During his political career, taken up in the 1950s, he has been Foreign Minister (1973–74) and the founder of the Mouvement des Démocrates (1974), while at the same time writing on political subjects: *Mémoires d'Avenir* (1974), *Les Idées Simples de la Vie* (1975), *L'Autre Regard* (1976), and *Parler aux Français* (1977).

ALFRED KASTLER. Nobel Prize in physics (1966) for his work on optical methods of magnetic resonance and 'optical pumping'. Has held a number of high university appointments, such as Professor of Science at the University of Paris, Director of Research at the French National Scientific Research Centre (CNRS) and Professor at the University of Louvain. Has been a member of the Institute of France (Academy of Sciences) since 1964, and is a member of a number of foreign academies.

VLADIMIR KEMENOV. Vice-President of the Soviet Academy of Fine Arts. Has written works on art and aesthetic history, such as *The Paintings of Velasquez* and *The Historical Paintings of Surikov*. Has been a member of the Executive Board of Unesco.

PREM KIRPAL. An Indian thinker. President of the Institute of Cultural Relations and Development Studies in New Delhi, a former university teacher, he has also been Director of Unesco's Department of Cultural Activities and a member of its Executive Board.

TCHAVDAR KURANOV. Bulgarian sociologist, the author of numerous publications, worked for the United Nations Economic Commission for Europe before becoming a Counsellor of State. Currently a research scientist at the Bulgarian Academy of Sciences, and Secretary-General of the Bulgarian Group for the Pugwash Conferences.

TAKEO KUWABARA. Professor of French Literature at the University of Kyoto, Director of the Institute of Human Sciences, a member of the Japanese National Commission for Unesco, he is a specialist in cultures and civilizations and the author of a number of studies on French literature.

SEAN MACBRIDE. Irish statesman, Chairman of Amnesty International. Formerly United Nations Commissioner for Namibia, he was awarded the Nobel Peace Prize in 1974.

MIRCEA MALITZA. A mathematician who is currently researching into games theory and mathematical models in the social sciences. A Professor at the University of Bucharest, and former Minister of Education, he has been entrusted with various missions to the United Nations and Unesco. Author of numerous works on mathematics and the social sciences, and also of studies on futurology.

M. L. MEHROTRA. A lung specialist, Director of the Tuberculosis Demonstration and Training Centre at Agra, has taken part in many preventive medicine campaigns. He is a member of professional societies in India and abroad.

HEPHZIBAH MENUHIN-HAUSER. American pianist, resident in London since 1957. In addition to her career as an artist, is actively involved in international co-operation in numerous fields.

PHILIP NOEL-BAKER. Has had a lengthy public career, both in the United Kingdom (Member of Parliament and a member of the Cabinet in various Labour governments), and on the international plane (from the League of Nations to the United Nations). He has lectured in various British and American universities, has written a number of books and articles (on international law, justice and peace), and was awarded the Nobel Peace Prize in 1959.

JEAN D'ORMESSON. A *professeur agrégé* in philosophy, has held a number of government appointments and attended various international conferences as a member of the French delegation. Since 1950, Secretary-General of the International Council for Philosophy and Humanistic Studies. The author of several novels and studies, he was elected to the French Academy in 1973.

ALICIA PENALBA. Argentine sculptor, whose impressive works are represented in a number of museums of contemporary art in Europe and the United States.

NANCY REEVES. A lawyer, and one of the leaders of the United States feminist movement. The author of a number of works on the status of women, she is actively involved in the work of numerous non-governmental organizations seeking to promote international co-operation and peace.

JANEZ STANOVNIK. Executive Secretary of the United Nations Economic Commission for Europe since 1968, has been successively Director of the Executive Office of the Vice-President and Foreign Minister of Yugoslavia, economic adviser to the permanent delegation of Yugoslavia in New York, Director of the Institute of International Politics and Economics, and professor of economics at the University of Ljubljana. In 1965 he was appointed special adviser to the Secretary-General at the United Nations Conference on Trade and Development (UNCTAD).

TRAN VAN KHE. Currently Director of Research at the French National Scientific Research Centre (CNRS), where he is conducting a comparative study on the musical language of Asian countries; he is President of the Scientific Committee of the Berlin International Institute for Comparative Music Studies and Documentation, and a member of the International Music Council (Unesco). Has contributed to several encyclopaedias of music, and written two works on traditional Vietnamese music, *La Musique Vietnamienne Traditionnelle* and *Vietnam, les Traditions Musicales*.

PETER USTINOV. Actor, dramatist, film director and writer, whose output is considerable both in its variety and in the originality of its style. One of his plays, *The Love of Four Colonels* has been seen all over the world. For nearly ten years now he has been actively involved in international co-operation in connection with Unicef and Unesco.

BERNARD ZEHRFUSS. A French architect, who has worked in various countries, in particular Tunisia. He is responsible for Unesco Headquarters in Paris, the French Embassy in Warsaw, the Archaeological Museum in Lyons, the New University in Tunis, and residential areas in Tunis, to quote only a few examples. Honorary member of the Institute of American Architects and of the Royal Society of Arts of Great Britain.